Worlds in Conflict

By the same author

POLITICAL PATTERNS IN TODAY'S WORLD

AMERICA IN THE MODERN WORLD

THE FRENCH NATION

AN INTRODUCTION TO AMERICAN POLITICS

THE PRICE OF REVOLUTION

AMERICAN THEMES

FRENCH PERSONALITIES AND PROBLEMS

THE FREE STATE

THE AMERICAN PROBLEM

THE ENGLISH PEOPLE

THE DEVELOPMENT OF MODERN FRANCE

THE AMERICAN POLITICAL SYSTEM

Worlds in Conflict

BY

D. W. BROGAN

Professor of Political Science and Fellow of Peterhouse in the University of Cambridge; Honorary Fellow of Corpus Christi College, Oxford; Fellow of the British Academy; Foreign Member of the Massachusetts Historical Society, the Institut de France, and the American Academy of Arts and Sciences

HAMISH HAMILTON

LONDON

First published in Great Britain 1967
by Hamish Hamilton Ltd
90 *Great Russell Street, London, WC*1

Printed in Great Britain by
Western Printing Services Ltd, Bristol

To

SUSAN STRANGE

Preface

THIS volume initiates the Jacob Blaustein Lectures in International Relations at Lehigh University.

The donor of this series, Mr. Jacob Blaustein, a leading American industrialist and philanthropist, has served as a member of the United States Delegation to the United Nations; was a member of President Truman's Mobilization Policy Board during the Korean War; and is a Consultant to the State Department on International Business Problems.

It is the purpose of the donor to present annually a distinguished scholar or statesman to deliver a series of lectures on an important subject of world politics and to have the lectures published in order to reach a wide audience.

We hope and believe that this first series, delivered by Sir Denis Brogan at Lehigh in March 1965, sets a high standard for the lectures which are to follow. Sir Denis Brogan, Professor of Political Science in the University of Cambridge, is widely recognized as a leading British authority on American affairs. His many books and articles on the United States have helped shape opinion on both sides of the Atlantic. This volume continues and extends his valuable contributions as a perceptive observer and critic of things American.

CAREY B. JOYNT
Professor and Head
Department of International Relations

Lehigh University
Bethlehem, Pennsylvania

Introduction

I

THE year that has passed since I gave the Blaustein lectures at Lehigh University has fully justified the prudence which I displayed in avoiding detailed prediction. Had I made any predictions, some would by this time have been proved to be absurdly wrong; others would have been proved to be absurdly inadequate; and some would have proved to be totally irrelevant. At the same time, so many events have occurred which I did not foresee, and could not have predicted, that it is quite obvious that any consideration of American foreign policy written today must be extremely tentative in its diagnoses, its recommendations and its predictions.

Reflecting on the present situation, it seems to me obvious that we are faced not with changes and modifications of the Cold War, but with something like the breakup of the ice in the springtime on a great American river or on the Volga. The barriers which the long winter has created, are coming down in every part of the world; the ice-floes are bumping against each other before dissolving; all the torrents released from the grip of winter are flowing with great and possibly dangerous speed in rather undefined directions. The waters pouring from the great streams are spreading over the landscape and it will be a long time before they settle and allow us to see again some permanent Mount Ararats, not only in Asia but all over the world.

It is even more obvious in 1966 than it was in 1965 that we are living under the Chinese curse, 'May you live in interesting times'; and it is not only we who are living under that curse: the Chinese are visibly living under it too. Only the most doctrinaire and conceited rulers or advisers of rulers can have any confidence that they know how the tide of history is moving. Political changes inconceivable a few months ago are visibly under way. Political structures that seemed fairly stable have collapsed. Hopes based, for example, on the spread of some form of democratic government in Latin America and in Africa are, in 1966, not held so firmly as they were in 1965. Historical phenomena of great consequence and ambiguous meaning like the clash between Russia and China are more interesting but less intelligible than ever. Nor are the changes in situations and in possibilities confined to the 'under-privileged countries'. On the agenda of history at the moment is the position in the world of Great Britain. In a year or two it may have changed as it has not changed since the eighteenth century, perhaps as it has not changed since the discovery of America made a small group of islands off the coast of Europe geographically one of the centres of the world. 'The British Commonwealth of Nations' may have gone the way of the British and the Roman Empires within the next year or two; and it is too early to decide whether such a disappearance of a comparatively new political organization is disastrous or merely a recognition of basic facts which no formula can alter.

Even in the most powerful political society of the world, the United States, change is visible and rapid. A great deal of the linguistic weaponry of the Cold War period is now unusable or, if used, is ineffective. The young people of the United States, like the young people of Europe, remember only vaguely the agonies of the Second World War, the doubts, hesitations, fears, and timid hopes of the post-war period. After all, it is twenty-one years since the Second World War ended—as long a period as between the opening of the French Revolution and the fall of Napoleon. As it would have been absurd to attempt to conduct the business of the Congress of Vienna in 1814 in terms of the state structure of 1789, it is absurd today to conduct the foreign policy of the United States in terms of 1945, of the ending of the Second War, of the dropping of the first atomic bombs, of the slow realization that if war was ended, peace had not arrived.

So the main lesson of my original lectures still seems valid. The American people (and of course the British, French, German, Russian, Chinese peoples) would be well advised to keep their 'options open' and keep their fingers crossed. Whatever the world may be like ten years from now, it is very unlikely that any predictions made today will prove to be right by that time. And again, it is hard for people who can remember, as I can, the First World War, to realize how remote it is in history, how ambiguous its results are, how many of those results have been unpleasant, how small a part of the population of a world of which most members do not remember the Second, much less the First World War, can be expected to think in terms which come as second nature to people of my generation, or even to younger people like the President of the United States, and to older people like the President of the French Republic.

Any political system based on the freezing of attitudes or the freezing of expectations of 1945 (however natural and wise those attitudes were in 1945) is doomed to be frustrating, fruitless, and possibly disastrous. The American government may still talk officially of 'the Republic of China', the Chiang Kai-shek régime on the island of Formosa; but it is seventeen years since the last remnants of the Kuomintang army took refuge on Formosa, a period as long as that between the election of Lincoln and the debated election of President Hayes which officially marked the end of the aftermath of the American Civil War. American politicians and, probably, the majority of the

American people conspicuously abandoned in 1877 their official programme of 'reconstruction' of the South, throwing their hand in with consequences which are visible today. We can see, in retrospect, how and why this happened. We can see how it was inevitable and politically necessary. It may be that, a hundred years from now, the abandonment of the rigidities of 1945 will seem as possibly mistaken as the abandonment of the hopes of 1865; but posterity must live to itself. As a wit said, 'Why should I care for posterity? What has posterity done for me?'

It is not only that the world is changing, and changing very rapidly. It would be astonishing if it did not change at a time when it is quite likely that man will soon be walking on the moon. Walking on the moon will not help and probably not hinder the development of a rational foreign policy or perhaps the development of a rational world order. But it is a little difficult to imagine that a world being technologically transformed, such as we observe today, can live on ideas inherited from the missionary effort in China of the late nineteenth and early twentieth centuries, or on political and military grievances created by the Treaty of Versailles or by the absence of a treaty in 1945. It may be, as General de Gaulle thinks, that states pursue only their interests and that certain states have permanent interests although they have no permanent enemies and no permanent friends, a view, it might be remembered, expressed by Lord Palmerston as the basis of English policy long before it became the open theory of French policy. It might be convenient if we *could* blot out all the historical past which clashes, in so many ways, with the technological present, but all we can do is to stress how much of the past we *must* accept, how much of the past we *must* deal with, and how much the influence of the past is compatible with the speed of change of a world going through the greatest revolution in its way of life since the discovery of fire. To repeat something I said in the body of my lectures, we must clear our minds of cant. We can wave the Stars and Stripes—or even the Stars and Bars. We can wave the Union Jack, forgetting that the union which it commemorated has been broken since 1921. We can wave the tricolour, forgetting that France no longer necessarily represents hope or 'liberty, equality, fraternity'. We can think it totally unnatural that Bismarck's *Reich* should be divided as it is divided, and yet that division may last a very long time—perhaps as long as Bismarck's *Reich* did. We can see that something new, something promising, something alarming, something dangerous is happening in Africa, is happening in Asia, is happening in Latin America; but we do not know from our point of view, or even from the point of view of the inhabitants of these so-called backward regions, what is going to happen and whether it will be promising, disastrous, or suicidal. We can be certain that political warfare, like military warfare, will never follow the plans laid down by any general staff, by any Pentagon, by any computer, and that what happens will contain vast elements of accident and vast elements of unpleasant surprises. The world cannot be made, by any exercise of American wisdom or power, a safe and agreeable place to live in. But it will be a safer world to live in if as much emotion as possible can be evacuated from our minds; and if some emotion remains—and some should remain—we must allow for its existence and allow for its consequences. We will have to decide—and not only the American people will have to decide—how much we in the West really mean the democratic slogans we mouth, how much we must appear as humbugs, and how much the rest of the world may perhaps be excusing its own faults and follies by pointing, truthfully enough, at our faults, our selfishness, and our misunderstanding of what the majority of the human race think they need, want, and deserve.

To call on the American people, on its leaders, on its pastors and masters for candour, self-control, self-criticism will strain American temper and shock American optimism. (Equally a reconstruction of the future rôle of Great Britain in the world may deeply shock patriotic attitudes and patriotic beliefs lying just below the surface of British public opinion.) The French, if not General de Gaulle, may learn a lot, learn the very serious limitations of French power and the differences of scale between France and the United States and the Soviet Union. Needless to say, the same self-examination, the same self-criticism, the same self-control are needed in their own interests, not only in ours, by the developing nations in Africa, Asia, and Latin America. The expense will be expense of temper as well as of treasure. There will be an expense of national vanity as well as of deep national pride. That will mean a reconstruction of religious, ethical, political and, one suspects, even sporting attitudes, in many countries which see themselves as victims, which they may be, and never as sinners, which they also are. It would be absurd to preach to the American people that because they are the most powerful body politic in the world, they must bear all the burden of the world's sins and all the world's responsibilities. They do not believe, and nobody could argue them into such a belief, in a general American guilt which they do not feel. But serious as are the faults and follies in Ghana or in the Argentine Republic, in Burma, or in Belgium, they are not as important as the faults and follies in the United States. And it is one of the merits of the American people, in their present temper, that they are very willing to hear of their own faults, to wonder about their own responsibilities even if they resent criticism from countries which have not managed their own affairs conspicuously well and whose deplorable economical and political position is not visibly the fault of the United States.

To return to the metaphor of the ice breaking up on the river, we are all in canoes shooting through the icy waters, dodging the ice-floes, making for the sea, hoping to get there but only vaguely conscious of how to do it or, indeed, of where the sea is. Rulers like Mao Tse-tung who *know* where the sea is, who know how to navigate rivers (or to swim them) and who, indeed, specialize in steering in various ways through dangerous waters, need have no such fears and no such doubts—or conceal them. The rivers that Mao Tse-tung navigates are for this very reason remarkably alarming phenomena. Better is the attitude of a ruler who is not one of my favourites, Oliver Cromwell, who told the Scottish ministers to consider that they might be mistaken. Cromwell occasionally thought that *he* might be mistaken. Some other rulers have admitted, after the event, that they have been very badly mistaken. For the American people ought to encourage in its rulers, and hope to see in the rulers of other countries, some of this Cromwellian spirit, some of that new questioning of the belief that American patriotism is an answer to all the needs of the American citizen. Patriotism is a virtue, not a vice; patriotism is perhaps necessary for the promotion of certain social virtues without which we cannot live together; but, as Nurse Cavell said in the First World War, before the Germans shot her, 'Patriotism is not enough', and this is a lesson for loyal citizens everywhere. No more in the White House and in the Capitol than in Westminster or in the Élysée is this a lesson only for America's rulers or only for the American people. But if weaker nations prove slow studies, as the actors put it, that is unfortunate; if the American people prove slow studies, that may be disastrous, and disastrous in a way to which past history provides no possibility of comparison.

II

The most important international events of the past year have been the changes in Chinese policy internally and externally. Internally, an upheaval has taken place of whose character and scale we are not yet competent to judge. Externally, China is more and more hostile to the outside world of the West *and* more and more hostile to Russia. Each of these attitudes is of great importance for American policy and for the foreign policy of America's allies. But it is essential that the American people and the American government should accept the awkward fact that the most important thing about China today is the continuation of the Chinese revolution, and that internal revolution may well be—is almost certain to be—far more important than any question of Chinese foreign policy or of the American tendency to see China—perhaps to see all outside powers—in terms of their impact on the United States. Even if there were no differences of opinion and policy between China and the United States; if there were no war in Vietnam; if China had no interest or part in that war; or if the United States had washed its hands of policy on the Asiatic mainland; the Chinese upheaval would still be the most important news story of these years.

As we can see, looking back on the First World War, the most important event was the Russian Revolution or, more specifically, the chance given to the small Bolshevik party to take over the revolution which might have occurred, and probably would have occurred in some form or other, anyway. It is probably too much to say that the taking over of the Chinese revolution (which had been going on since before the First World War) by the Chinese Communist Party of Mao was the most important result of the Second World War—I do not think that it was; but I accept the possibility that it may turn out to have been the most important result.

If it proves to be the case that Mao has successfully broken with the Confucian and Taoist past, that he has cut China off from its European teachers and aggressors (among whom Russia is of course to be counted), there is a *prima facie* ground for asserting that if the Second World War alone made this takeover bid possible, the success of this bid is the most important result of that war.

There are obvious objections to any such theory. A victory of Hitler would also have been a victory for Japan, and a victorious Japan might have been able to prevent the Communist takeover bid in 1949, as a victorious Germany would have been able to undo the Communist takeover bid in Russia in 1918–19. The China that Mao took over was poor, backward, disunited, and in all probability from the economic and military points of view a 'paper tiger'. But nevertheless it can hardly be doubted that the most important *positive* result of the Second World War, apart from the destruction of the Nazi and Japanese empires, was the taking over of China by a Chinese Communist Party based on a tradition of peasant revolt, not on the seizure of power in the cities by a small, trained, revolutionary élite.

The Communists in China had used their power in the countryside to seize the cities; whereas the Communists in Russia used the power they had acquired in towns and cities to enforce their rule on the countryside. Professor Walt Rostow has insisted on the importance of the fact that 'Marx was a town boy', and the repeated failures of Marxian agricultural policy in Russia and all over the Russian dependencies in Europe justifies this comment. But Mao was and is a country boy, not by origin and education, but by his experience as a revolutionary leader. The transformation, if it has taken place, of a quarter of the human race on the doctrinal lines laid down by Chairman Mao may be quite as important as the transformation of Russia by Lenin. It may also be original, for Lenin was a Westerner in education and bias, whereas it is obvious that one of the strengths (possibly also the weaknesses) of Chairman Mao is that he combines a formal allegiance to Marxism-Leninism-Stalinism with the profound Chinese belief in the superiority of China and the

Chinese, a superiority going far back into history and certain to go far into the future. Lenin, after all, placed his hopes on a Communist revolution in Germany, to which the Russian Revolution was a mere curtain-raiser. Mao has placed, and more and more places his hopes and plans in a Chinese revolution which adheres less and less in its ideological form to the West, to Russia, to Europe, to the United States. It is important to bear this truth constantly in mind, for we may be deceived by drum-beating from Peking, by threats, by explosions and by temper, by prophecies of the future triumph of the peasant countries of the world over industrialized societies, an imitation in history of the Communist capture of the Chinese cities by the Chinese countryside. But common sense suggests that the rulers of China and the people of China are more concerned at the moment with the fate of Mao's doctrines and practices than they are concerned with the fate of a Maoist revolutionary triumph outside China itself.

It is easy to assert—for it is true—that the Chinese Communist export movement has failed for the moment. It has failed disastrously and conspicuously in Indonesia; and in a continent where so many people, very wisely, plan to back a winner, the savage penalties inflicted on those Indonesians who backed a loser, i.e. the Chinese Communist-directed revolution, is highly educational. Maoism may be the wave of the future all over Asia—this is not at all impossible, and, as some people argue, is highly likely; but it is a wave which at the moment is receding. And if this is true of Asia, it is still more true of Africa and of Latin America. The great siege of the urbanized, capitalist, or deviationist world by the rural masses led by the Chinese Communists has not yet begun. It may never begin. For the moment, unless the rulers of China have completely lost the caution which in many ways they have displayed since they triumphed in 1949, their real attention is being devoted to whatever is going on in China.

'Hawks' and 'Doves' have far more interest in discovering what is the present state of the continuing Chinese revolution than they have in guessing what military activities China is fostering in Vietnam or threatening against India. To repeat a platitude, Mao and his colleagues rule a fourth of the human race, and they may wish, and may be forced by events, to retreat into that self-imposed isolation which has marked 'the Middle Kingdom' at several times in its history.

For these reasons, it is more important than ever not only to discard such tattered rags of the old illusions about the Kuomintang, about 'the loss of China', about the betrayal of the Chinese revolution, but to think of the 'Chinese problem' as above all a problem in internal politics and policy and only indirectly—and possibly in a very minor degree—a question of foreign policy. It is obviously convenient for the rulers of China to persuade the rulers of the United States that China is as much a menace for world order as were, for example, Hitler's Germany and militarist Japan. But this may be a necessity in diverting the attention of the rulers of America, and even the rulers of Britain, from the realities of the Chinese situation, from the problems which any rulers of China will have to face.

It is possible to argue, and it has been argued powerfully, that the new China of Mao is economically and militarily a paper tiger. It is possible to argue that China is in fact an intrinsically poor country and that it is 'overextended', not in territorial area, but in its demographic aspects. That is to say, the fact that the Chinese are a quarter of the human race—and soon may be a higher proportion—may be a handicap and not a help. To become a modern, industrial state, China, like all other countries in the past, will have to squeeze surplus value out of the peasants to provide the capital for an adequate programme of industrialization. But there may be no surplus to be squeezed out of the peasants because there are too many peasants. Mao can preach an austerity programme; he may not only, as is very likely, be reaffirming his belief in the virtues developed during the Long March and during the war against the Kuomintang; he may be as ready to preach and practise a doctrine of 'frugal plenty', with the emphasis on the frugal, as was Mr. de Valera in what now seems a remote past in modern Ireland. But his hand may now be forced by the problems of population, by the birth rate, by the comparatively meagre resources of Chinese territory compared with the needs of the Chinese people. True, the problem has been traditionally also a Japanese problem, and statistically speaking, is still a Japanese problem that looks more serious than the Chinese problem. But the Japanese are not so much handicapped by vanity, by unwillingness to learn or by being ruled by a classical Chinese poet, as are the Chinese.

What is the point of these rather banal remarks? It is merely to suggest that the great upheaval now going on in China may be of great importance for the immediate present, and perhaps still more for the future of China, but may have no immediate importance for the policy of the United States. It may be that Mao is swimming over another waterfall, to adjust a famous English proverbial expression;[1] or, to go back to a Chinese metaphor much used a few years ago, he may be making another 'great leap forward' and may fall on his face again, as he did then. The

[1] As we all know, Chairman Mao at 72 swims in a way that would fill with envy young Australian Olympic swimmers. Cynics may think that the report of the Chairman's swimming feats recalls the joke played on Theodore Roosevelt at the Republican Convention in Chicago of 1912 where there was found one morning on every seat in the convention hall a card announcing 'Theodore Roosevelt will walk on the waters of Lake Michigan at 3 o'clock this afternoon'. Indeed, a great deal of what comes out of China and is reported with irony by the Russian press recalls some of the most nonsensical of American and other political campaigns and a degree of divinizing of the head of the state that might have turned the stomach even of Stalin or Mussolini.

policy now being preached and practised by the organized strenuous youth movements of China, may be a policy designed to cover up resentment and hostility to many aspects of the remaking of Chinese society which have been so much admired by Westerners who would be horrified to see any such society created in their own countries. It may be, as has often been suggested, that Chairman Mao is anguished by the thought that the austerity, discipline, and devotion which the Chinese Communist Party displayed in such abundance, and which produced in many aspects of Chinese life very impressive results, have now become unpopular and possibly impracticable. 'The mandate of Heaven' may be in the process of being withdrawn from Chairman Mao. I do not think this is likely; but some great subterranean earthquake *is* occurring, and all that political seismologists can do is to register the internal quakes, landslips, and possibly volcanic explosions—and to remember that these are far more important for the Chinese governors and governed than any external triumphs.

It may be, of course, that Chairman Mao and his heir apparent Marshal Lin Piao do intend to divert the Chinese people from the maladies and agonies of an even more profound transformation of traditional Chinese society than they have endured in the last twenty years. The Communist leaders have not, in fact, shown themselves to be nearly as much tempted by these diversions as the Fascist leaders were. Neither Lenin nor Stalin, although they used nationalist fervour and nationalist feeling, ever launched out on dangerous, merely nationalist adventures as did Mussolini and Hitler and the rulers of Japan in the years before Pearl Harbor. And it may be that the ideological isolationism by which the Mao régime is now displaying its contempt for the alleged advanced countries, its conviction that, as in the past, so in future, China will set the norm of human achievement, will save the rulers of China from the temptation to adventure which ruined other dictatorial régimes in this century. We may be sure that, however archaic are the military theories of Marshal Lin, however much he may believe in the superiority of his mass armies, he does not believe any longer that the United States is a paper tiger; and he may very well hesitate to launch out on a course of action in which the reality of the tiger's claws will be decided.

In any event, we may be certain that control of China, with the harnessing of the forces released by the new campaign for saving the soul of the Chinese Communist revolution, preoccupies the rulers of China and the people of China much more even than does Vietnam or North Korea, or the wickedness of Russia or the impotence of the United States. And just as the policy of China is certainly not centred exclusively or mainly on the problem of relations with the United States, it will probably be wise for the rulers of the United States and the American people not to see in Communist China the cause of all their ills, and in its defeat and destruction the remedy for those ills, ills inherent, as I have argued elsewhere, in the human situation and not in the particular wickedness of societies which are refusing to adopt the American Way of Life.

III

It is against this background of the great internal upheavals in China, of the vicissitudes and the transformation of China, which may take another generation before more than the outlines are visible, that the American people should consider the problem of 'Vietnam'. As I argued in the lectures I gave last year, the Americans have inherited in Vietnam a series of problems which they did not create. It is easy enough to dismiss these problems as the results of the nefarious rule of France for fifty years or so. This is to take too simplified a view of East Asiatic history, and too simplified a theme of 'imperialism'. In many ways, modern Vietnam is a French creation. It could be argued, indeed, that the destruction of French rule in what they called Indo-China has been a disaster as it has brought to the surface a number of problems which the French had at any rate managed to control from roughly 1870 onwards. It is easy to see the movement southward of the militant Tongkingese as simply a Communist conspiracy inspired, subsidized, directed from China. It is easy to see everything that is displeasing in the states of what was the French Union of Indo-China as weaknesses which are due to imperial rule. But many of these problems date from long before any French people had ever heard of Indo-China.

The great ruins of Angkor Vat, which General de Gaulle has recently been visiting, should have some of the educational effect of contemplating the wreck of the statue of Ozymandias, King of Kings. Just as the country round Delhi is covered with the ruins of empty or degraded imperial capitals, so are the cities of what was Indo-China full of historical relics whose ghosts haunt the policy of the United States, as they haunted the policy of France.

To act on the Johnsonian maxim, 'Clear your mind of cant', is to be forced to admit that a good many of the problems now facing the United States as the new imperial power are more or less the same as those that faced France as the old imperial power. Just as President George Washington found himself faced with many of the problems of the American frontier that were too much for King George III, so the new imperial power, the United States, is faced with many of the problems which became too much for the French after the collapse of France in Europe and the destruction of their power and prestige by the Japanese between 1940 and 1945.

One of the most eminent and wisest students of East Asia did inform the Foreign Relations Committee of the

United States Senate that although the Americans were sleeping in the French bed, they were not dreaming the French dreams. First of all, sleeping in anybody's bed can have awkward consequences, even if there are no dreams. Secondly, how do we know that the inhabitants of what was French Indo-China know what dreams the Americans are dreaming or think that they differ in any important way from the French dreams? And how do we know that the Americans are not dreaming new dreams as illusory as, and doomed to a shorter life than the dreams of such makers of the French colonial empire in Indo-China as Paul Bert, Jules Ferry, Albert Sarraut, and the Admiral Thierry d'Argenlieu? One of the alarming features of a great deal of the official output of reassuring messages from the White House and the Pentagon is the verbal resemblance to what the French were saying from 1945 until they threw their hand in in 1954. The same possibly insoluble problems produce the same comforting noises.

Of course, the noises made by the Pentagon or even by the White House are more comforting and more plausible than those made in Paris or in Saigon by the French. The United States is not a defeated country and has overwhelming resources which the French lacked. Until quite recently, it had the great advantage of not appearing necessarily as an imperial power opposing a strong, indigenous, nationalist movement. The strong nationalist movement was threatening French power, feebly it is true, before the last war. One of the first agitators who was in at the birth of the French Communist Party after the First War was the young Annamite student, Ho Chi-minh. Whatever chances the French had of adjusting themselves to a dignified retreat from Indo-China such as the British achieved in India, they lost very largely through the imperious temper of Thierry d'Argenlieu, the monk turned admiral, but still more through the refusal of the French to accept the obvious consequences of British withdrawal; for if the

British had to leave a far greater, richer, more powerful imperial position, held firmly for a much longer period, it was impossible to believe that the French in Indo-China (or the Dutch in Java) could succeed where the British had failed, or where the British had voluntarily given up their imperial rôle, whichever way we care to look at it.

The French failed not only to convince the revolutionary leaders, north and south, in Tongking and Cochin-China, of their good faith; they did not display good faith. And, contrasting with the last years of French rule, the American assistance to the political and economic well-being of Vietnam could possibly have seemed not a new form of imperialism but a specialized form of American aid. Whether this was a practical policy or not, no one will ever know. For by the time the French threw in their hand in 1954 and the Americans picked it up, it was a bad hand with very few trumps.

It is for this reason that so many of the official *apologias* from the White House and the Pentagon sound like the old French stories. The crisis of credibility which destroyed what little willingness the French people had to continue the 'dirty war' is now raging in the United States, as I discovered on a very recent visit. There is, in fact, far more disbelief just below the surface, among people whose disbelief is quite serious, than has yet been overtly declared.

It is now evident that one of the difficulties which the French inherited or invented is now plaguing the Americans. In India, for all their faults, the British had trained at Oxford and Cambridge, Sandhurst and in gaol, a ruling class for both India and what became Pakistan. It is possible that Ho Chi-minh could have become another Nehru if a great many things that did not happen had happened. But the weakness of the French position between 1950 and 1954 was above all political. The policy of bringing back the former emperor of Annam, Bao Dai, to be a rallying centre of nationalism, traditionalism and the political base for an amicable settlement with France, was not intrinsically foolish. Of course, Bao Dai was not a leader of anything like the intelligence or energy of Ho Chi-minh. His dynasty had not such deep traditional roots as many of the French seem to have thought. But above all, he was not given a chance to 'make like an emperor'. The French did not even build up the traditional, ornamental, sacred character of the office to which they wished to restore Bao Dai. Even had his imperial authority and prestige not been weakened by his loss of all plausibility as a ruler under the Japanese, it would have required a great deal of political talent on the French side and political talent among the counsellors of the emperor to make this experiment succeed. And it was the political failure which doomed the French military effort. For it must be remembered that no indigenous South Vietnamese force, or, so far, any American force, has had such military successes as were achieved by Marshal de Lattre de Tassigny. But Marshal de Lattre and Marshal Leclerc, following up the principles of Marshal Foch, realized that the basic problem in Indo-China was not military, but political.[1]

The problem which faced the French faces the Americans. The governmental structure they are backing in what is now called South Vietnam is less and less plausible. There, it is not a crisis of credibility, but of the virtually universal prevalence of incredibility. It is conceivable that Diem was the best ruler in the American sense that they could find for South Vietnam. If that is so, the experiment of creating a state and an alleged nation called South Viet-

[1] We now know that in 1919 Marshal Foch refused to send troops to the debatable land between renascent Poland, the Ukraine, Great Russia, Hungary—all the fragmented relics of the broken-down empires. He asked was there a government to support? And being told there was no such government, he replied, 'A government can get along without an army, but an army cannot get along without a government'.

nam was doomed from the start. But it is also obvious that no successor has been found for Diem, that the decline of political effort by the Vietnamese state has been catastrophic and has been reflected not only in politics, but in war. The young man who calls himself Marshal Ky is quite clearly a very inferior version of a traditional mandarin like Diem, but may not be so much handicapped by religious associations as was the zealous Diem and his much too zealous brother, the Archbishop of Hué. But it is very difficult, indeed, to see what is the claim of Marshal Ky on the support of his fellow-countrymen, a claim that begs a great many questions in any case, and on the government of the United States. It is certainly not due to any known military achievements. That he is tough, brave, anti-Communist, and all the other adjectives beloved by *Time* magazine is no doubt true. Anti-Communism, like patriotism, is not enough.[1]

It is because of these, I should have thought, extremely obvious considerations that it is rash to parallel the situation of the government set up in and around Saigon (this seems to be the best description of it) with a gallant little nation striving to protect its independence, its culture, etc., etc. There is no visibly viable body politic in South Vietnam, and there is less and less, at the moment of writing, evidence of an effective fighting force. From the point of view of its supporters as well as its enemies, the United States in Vietnam today is not merely in the French bed; it is behaving in that bed in the same way that the French did.

To say this is not to condemn, by this parallel, all

[1] The rôle of Marshal Ky is rather like a parody of the rôle in his last active years of Generalissimo Chiang Kai-shek. 'Why', asked Senator Tom Connelly, Chairman of the Foreign Relations Committee of the United States Senate, 'if he is a generalissimo doesn't he generalize?' One could put the same question to Marshal Ky, and one need not stay for an answer.

American action. The Americans are discovering, to their astonishment, that a great deal of what the French did in Indo-China was worth doing, and that a great many of the Indo-Chinese in North and South Vietnam, in Cambodia and Laos, are very much more deeply marked by their French training than they are likely to be by any American training. Even the enemies of French rule opposed French rule in a French way. So it does not follow that the Americans are doomed to fail in Vietnam simply because they are, by necessity, in many ways imitating the French; in some ways imitating the French better, and in some ways imitating them worse. And the immense economic and military resources of the United States make it possible that they can do a great deal to repair the damage that more than twenty years of war have caused in Indo-China (an increasing amount of damage being caused by the Americans themselves).

But it is a very dangerous illusion to think that what is being defended in South Vietnam is an established, rational, deeply-rooted small nation 'rightly struggling to be free', or to remain free. Such a nation may be created in the future. The unity running from the Chinese border down to the borders of Malaysia which existed in 1939 was a French creation. It does not follow therefore that the area on the Mekong delta which the French called Cochin-China could not be turned into a state with as good prospects of survival as, say, Thailand. Even so, it would be under constant threat from the North where the energetic Tongkingese covet the fertile lands of the South. As a famous if bogus patriotic Welsh poem puts it,

> The mountain sheep are sweeter,
> But the valley sheep are fatter;
> We therefore deemed it meeter
> To carry off the latter.

Of course, these habits can be changed. The country round

Glasgow is far safer from Highland enterprise of this kind than it was in the time of Professor Adam Smith. The threats across the Afghan border are less serious than they were in the time of the British Raj. The economic prospects of South Vietnam, given peace, could be, by Asiatic standards, very good. But this is the point to insist on: only the clouding of counsel is produced by rhetorical references implausibly comparing the present of this former French colony with the past of, let us say, Scotland, Switzerland—or even the rebellious colonies of 1776. It is a rational political policy much more than a rational military policy that America most needs now.

What is, in the circumstances, a 'rational political policy'? Perhaps no rational political policy is possible. The late Lord Morley, the eminent Liberal intellectual, used to say that one of the hardest lessons to learn in politics is that there are often no good solutions, only less bad solutions. It seems to me quite certain that there is no good solution of the type contemplated, one assumes, by John Foster Dulles in 1954. That is to say, there will be no South Vietnamese state committed emotionally, ideologically, by gratitude, by necessity, to follow the policies of the United States in Asia, and still less in the world. Without having any inside or, indeed, much outside knowledge, I believe it to be certain that the inhabitants of this unfortunate portion of the globe would settle for the departure of the Americans, of the inhabitants and soldiers of North Vietnam, of the Vietcong and the various military leaders in South Vietnam in return for almost any kind of peace. Many of them would probably settle for the return of the French—at any rate, for the return of the French régime as it was in 1939. Americans tend to exaggerate the ideological commitment of people and to see the world, not only in black and white terms, but feel that people should and do prefer to live up to the assertion 'Give me liberty or give me death' without at this moment deciding what 'liberty' means in this context. It should be pointed out that when Patrick Henry made, or is declared to have made, this choice he was in no danger of Death and in no particular danger of losing his Liberty. In one form or another, the whole country that was French Indo-China has been suffering the horrors of war since 1940. The whole of Tongking, Annam, and Cochin-China has been suffering the horrors of war with hardly any interruption and on an increasingly horrible scale since 1953. In these circumstances, it is extremely unlikely that the luckless peasantry of this unfortunate region (for that is all it can be called at the moment) are as zealous in defence of the West or as undying anti-Communists as one would infer from reading *Time* magazine. There are times in history in which people prefer peace to justice, even when justice is an evident and realizable ideal.

Therefore, a rational political policy must begin by accepting the inevitable and natural desire of the people of South Vietnam—and one suspects of North Vietnam too—not to be liberated or defended at an excessively high cost. It also involves acceptance of the fact that the neighbours of Vietnam, North and South, may have many more important things to think about, from their benighted point of view, than saving the Western position or the American way of life in South-East Asia. In offering to defend South Vietnam, as a short time ago in threatening to liberate North Vietnam, the Americans are not necessarily in a seller's market. If the departure of the Americans would end the war, it is quite likely that a great part of the population of North and South Vietnam would gladly settle for tyranny. In the same way, it is equally probable that the inhabitants of North Vietnam would settle for peace even if it involved breaking with China or possibly even if it involved discarding its liberator Ho Chi-minh. I have no doubt that he is regarded as much more of a liberator than Chiang Kai-shek was regarded in China in his last disastrous years, or than Syngman Rhee ever was in Korea. But again the people of North Vietnam may find that being reconstructed on Communist lines has become a very expensive luxury. (Of course the departure of the Americans might make it a cheap luxury and one, if not necessarily appreciated, to be tolerated as very much better than war.)

This does not mean that a great deal of propaganda about liberating South Vietnam which comes from Communist organizations in Hanoi, from Moscow, from Peking is truthful. The war in Vietnam would have been ruthless even if the Americans had never entered it. It might well have been ruthless even if the French had never entered it. There is no reason to believe that the Tongkingese, a very militant and aggressive people, would not have been as formidable in totally local civil war as Chairman Mao and his Chinese have proved to be. There is no reason to doubt that such a war would have to be carried on with a savagery which we are accustomed, offensively and possibly hypocritically, to call 'Oriental'. The Catholic missionaries and converts in Hué in the middle of the nineteenth century were treated with an ingenious savagery which is indigenous although, of course, not unique.[1]

[1] Even the most devoted defenders of the régime of Ho Chi-minh and of the activities of what the Americans call the Vietcong do not deny that many acts of extreme savagery have been committed by the would-be liberators of South Vietnam. Thus, Lord Russell (*The Times*, September 30, 1966) blandly differentiates 'the violence of an oppressed people from that of the overwhelmingly powerful invader'. This apparently justifies any means that this oppressed people may use. Without going into the morals of this question, one might point out that this extravagant version of 'the end justifies the means' has been tried out in Europe. A good many Irishmen at the time of 'the Troubles' and many more since have realized that, horrible as were the methods of the British government under that eminent Liberal, Lloyd George, some of the methods used in retaliation were equally horrible and left scars on Irish life which are only now beginning to fade. No one who knows anything of the *épuration* of alleged collaborators in France in the period from August 1944 to, say, May 1945 can be quite

But if it is wise and right to reprove the savagery by which the Vietcong attempt to liberate and to impose their authority on South Vietnam, it is quite another thing to justify American adoption of equally savage means. Indeed, one could say more savage means, since the technical resources for horror in the hands of the Americans are greater than those in the hands of the Vietcong. There is another point. The American government says that in South Vietnam it is defending Western values. This means that it must fight with one hand tied behind its back. If it does not tie one hand behind its back, that is to say, *does* imitate its enemies (who do not profess Western values) and uses its immense technical superiority with no adequate sense of restraint, its crusading rôle is even more ambiguous and even less likely to be believed in. The French attempt in Algeria to defend Western values and formal democracy was perhaps doomed from the beginning. Yet it was not, formally speaking, a totally mean concept or a totally base objective. But when the French army imitated

as calm as is Lord Russell about the total results of such rough justice. The old revolutionary question, 'And was this blood so pure?' reveals an attitude of mind which is more natural and more defensible in rural Wales where Lord Russell lives than it would be in Auvergne where memories of the application of this principle are still lively, and one surmises than it would be in either Saigon or Hanoi. But as an admirer of Lord Russell's style, when I read a sentence justifying the blowing up of the restaurant in Saigon because it was 'a place habituated by senior American officers', I comfort myself with the view that perhaps Lord Russell is not the sole author of the letter he has signed. And when he is so confident that he knows exactly who is guilty in Vietnam, I am reminded of the fact that in his admirable book on his parents, *The Amberley Papers*, he reveals that his father, Lord Amberley, wanted to put on trial as war criminals the authors of the Franco-Prussian War of 1870; but the authors he wanted to put on trial were Napoleon III, Gramont, and Émile Ollivier. This was a judgement which I believe few historians today would think justified. Perhaps recent judgements by Lord Russell share some of his father's too rapid dogmatism.

and equalled and perhaps surpassed the Fellagha in savagery, the formal battle was won at the loss of the political and moral battle. 'The battle of Algiers' was indeed a Pyrrhic victory. So may many of the American battles turn out to be.

There are two points which the American people quite naturally do not notice about the exercise of American power in Vietnam. First, all of Asia is conscious of the fact that the atomic bomb was dropped on an Asiatic people and not on the Germans. Many believe (I do not) that had Germany still been in the war when the atomic bomb was ready, Germany would not have been induced to surrender by the atomic bomb.[1] But it is not merely a question of the dropping of the atomic bomb on an Asiatic people—to put it more brutally, on a coloured people. It is a question of the comparative immunity with which the Americans can do it.

An awkward truth which is accepted all over Europe as well as Asia, is that the lavish use of air power in Vietnam is the work of a country which has never been bombed and which, in this sense, does not know what it is doing. For this reason, a good deal of the American reporting of the war in Vietnam strikes people—for instance, in London—as odious. How it strikes them in Calcutta or Tokyo is a matter of speculation, but not of much doubt. If we contrast the resources of the United States and the resources of the Vietcong, whatever we may think of the political morality of the activities of the Vietcong, it does not seem to the outsider that the Vietcong are inferior to the Americans in courage, resolution, or belief in their cause. For this reason the news that the Americans had dropped napalm on their

[1] By accident, I lunched with the editorial staff of the *New York Times* in the week in which it was announced that the atomic bomb had been dropped. I and one other were the only people who defended the American action. I now think that I and the other minority member were wrong.

own troops was received with very mixed feelings in Europe. There were, of course, professional and permanent anti-Americans who had all the joys of *Schadenfreude* at the news. For them, there is no folly and no crime of which the Americans are not intrinsically capable, and there is no folly and no crime which the enemies of the Americans are not justified in committing. But many people who do not share these views in the least could not help reflecting that a fate had befallen unfortunate young American soldiers that has frequently befallen even more unfortunate Vietnamese children. This is part of the political cost of the use of American overwhelming technical power in a war of this kind. It is perhaps the only way the United States can wage this war, but this fact has to be put on the debit side of the bookkeeping of this war.[1] Therefore, all military news of successes from Vietnam (and much of the military news of successes has been false) is important only if that success prevents political defeat or leads to political victory. Certain kinds of success might lead to political defeat. There have been suggestions, for example, of destroying the elaborate dyke system of North Vietnam. For a country which depends on irrigation, such destruction would be an unforgivable and unforgiven crime—possibly as unforgiven in South Vietnam as in North. It was noted by Thucydides as a proof of the increasing barbarism of the Peloponnesian War that the Spartans occupying Attica destroyed the vineyards and the olives. For this they were not forgiven by the masses of the Athenian population. (They

[1] In all these questions, the American public is curiously insensitive. For example, a great many Europeans are not admirers of Dr. Wernher von Braun, and the fact that he is now working for the American government, as he worked for Hitler, is neither here nor there. So it was that when the film glorifying Dr. von Braun, *He aims at the Stars*, was shown in London, a reviewer succinctly commented, 'He aimed at the stars—but he hit London'. Every political use of American air power starts with at least one strike against it: it comes from a country which has been and is immune to the same kind of action.

were, of course, forgiven by the aristocratic and wealthy Athenians who saw the Spartans as allies, as perhaps some selfish and wealthy South Vietnamese would forgive the Americans.) And it took the French peasant a very long time to forgive the wanton destruction of trees, fields, crops, the seeds of future crops, committed by the Germans in their retreat in the spring of 1917. We may be sure that there are many people in the Pentagon and in the State Department who, quite apart from arguments of political advantage, know what a moral disaster total war waged even for the visibly best of causes in Vietnam would be; and for a great part of the human race, the cause is not visibly the best.[1]

There is no reason to believe that the American people are willing to use all their power in so ambiguous a cause as backing the alleged nation of South Vietnam or even backing the large number of South Vietnamese who very much object to being liberated by North Vietnam or by China, either directly or indirectly. I do not think the American conscience is at all easy on these points, and the more flag-waving and patriotic politicians and the noisier military men do not represent anything like the national consensus. Nor is it likely that they could by any propaganda methods create one.

No doubt there is a kind of victory the United States could win. 'They make a solitude and call it peace', said the Roman historian of Roman policy in Scotland nearly two thousand years ago, quoting a Caledonian leader of the time. The world has remembered the epigram more than it has remembered the pacification and semi-civilization of the Scottish Lowlands. The United States has to live in a world of which the overwhelming majority is suspicious of

[1] The announcement by General Eisenhower that he had been prepared to drop atomic bombs to induce the Chinese to make a treaty over Korea has shocked more people in Europe than perhaps the General realizes.

all imperial powers, of whom, in their possibly misguided way, they think the United States is one. It is a permanent problem of American diplomacy that has always to be taken into consideration when the question of immediate 'victory' or 'defeat' is being debated. No military victory without a political victory has any real meaning in this connexion, and some military methods make a political victory totally impossible. The United States, if it really wants to win in a realistic sense, *must* fight with a hand tied behind its back, and that means that the war must make greater and greater drains not only on American surplus wealth, but on American manhood and American temper. There is a price for victory in Vietnam—military victory or political victory—which is too high for the American people to be willing to pay it.

But is there anything short of complete victory and an ostentatious public defeat of what is assumed to be Chinese aggression? There is no way which is not too expensive to force North Vietnam or the Vietcong or China or all three of them together to accept a conspicuous defeat which would make the wavering peoples of South-East Asia confident that by backing, or being backed by the Americans they are on the winning side. The most that the United States could hope to gain by, say, 1967, is the production of an extremely delicate infant body politic which we could call South Vietnam for perhaps ten years. During these ten years, it may prove viable or wither on the vine. It may prove to be a successful rescue operation like, for example, the saving of the Philippines from 'the Huks', a success unappreciated in America because the power of the Huk rebels was not reported adequately to the American people when it was in full force. It may, on the other hand, turn out to be a version of the French attempt to set up Maximilian as Emperor of Mexico. That failed for many reasons, but for one basic one: that the United States, its hands freed by the ending of the Civil War, was close at hand and France was far away. When and if China gets through its present convulsions, it will be close at hand and the United States will be far away.

This, of course, as I say elsewhere, works both ways. In South-East Asia there is not only a millenary tradition of Chinese power; there is a millenary suspicion of Chinese power. The traditional heroes of some of these people were heroes because they resisted Chinese power. It is even more complicated than that, for the minor states of what the French called Indo-China, for example Laos and Cambodia, are more afraid of North Vietnam and South Vietnam than they are of China. They are also more afraid of Thailand than they are of China, and they are probably less afraid of the United States than of any of these rivals. It does not follow therefore that the failure of the American equivalent of Maximilian, whoever he may be—and Maximilian was quite as good a bet as Marshal Ky seems to be—will necessarily be Communist or, if Communist, will necessarily be a satellite of Chinese power.

In any event, we do not know what Chinese power will mean in the next few years. The present upheaval may mean no more than an attempt to get back to the austere and revered virtues of the early years of Chairman Mao's career, and the early years of the Chinese Communist Party. The present cultural revolution may be 'an experiment noble in purpose'—like Prohibition in America, to compare great things with small. Or it may produce convulsions that will keep China out of any active external policy for what is, by our standards, but not by Chinese standards, a long time. In the year 2000, to repeat myself, China will still *be* there and the United States will still not *be* there. Nothing can be done to alter the fact that Cuba is only 90 miles from Florida. That is more of a threat to Castro than to the United States. Canton is more than 90 miles from Hanoi, but it is much nearer than Washington. So in the political bookkeeping I am suggesting the United

States must employ some highly competent, perhaps foreign, bookkeepers to make the assessment. (Unfortunately many American bookkeepers are already committed to an optimistic view of the accounts.) The inevitable running down of American assets and the almost inevitable improvement of Chinese assets have got to be allowed for. Nothing in the not very long run, except an extraordinarily improbable collapse of China, can make the contest for power and influence in South-East Asia between the United States and China an equal affair. It can be made a nearly equal affair only on one condition, and that means that the United States manages to present itself to the peoples rather than to the states of South-East Asia as an ally against Chinese preponderance. And that means the United States must accept them as allies largely on their terms, not on American terms. For example, they may genuinely call themselves Communists, or they may simply use the word as a general 'boss word'. The American people must learn not to react automatically with horror at the mere mention of the word Communist. But those who use the word Communist in America and in Europe in a friendly sense may be very friendly indeed, seeing the Communists' triumph *ipso facto* as a triumph of the good. I have no such illusions; but preventing a country, for example South Vietnam or Cambodia, from going Communist should not be the main object of American policy even if it is feared that if one of these small states goes Communist, all the other states will, on the domino theory, fall.

The American people will have to accept the fact that, for good or ill, the Communists often represent in all of these countries the most energetic, active, and, from the point of view of character, admirable members of the society. In societies so archaic, with the old order breaking down and the new order not appearing, for the really patriotic and public-spirited young to go Communist is very tempting. This, of course, is true not only of Asia but of Latin America, and it must be allowed for. If it is not allowed for, the United States may find itself allied with people who are not very admirable in themselves, with people who have the naïve political ideas and ideals of Marshal Ky and are destined in the not very long run to fail. Every attempt that is made to save a part of 'the free world' from Communism should be undertaken only after a careful assessment of what is being saved. Thus, at the moment of writing, the United States has saved the Dominican Republic from the alleged danger of a Communist takeover. But for reasons which escape me, it has not managed to save Haiti, the other part of the island of Hispaniola, from a government much worse than any Communist government could possibly be.

Then it must also be remembered that in all of these regions there are many political problems that have nothing to do with even nominal Communism. Ghosts walk all the time. The ghosts may be absurd ghosts that one would have thought long dead. But that does not matter; they walk.[1]

The most the United States can hope for, it seems to me, in South Vietnam is the creation of a minimum political structure which promises peace first of all. Not peace on any terms, but peace on nearly any terms. It is possible but unlikely that the United States, by doubling its present military effort and by ignoring all political costs, can win a military victory and establish some kind of government supported by American military power. The claims of this government to represent any respectable political organization will deceive nobody outside the United States, and will deceive fewer and fewer people inside the United

[1] For example, I am not sure that the disciples of the Reverend Ian Paisley in Ulster, who are devoted to saving Ulster from Rome, would not prefer to be ruled by Chairman Mao rather than by Mr. Lemass; and the world is full of Ulsters.

States. Many Americans, possibly most Americans, feel this, and some see it clearly enough.

There are, of course, special obstacles in South Vietnam. For example, in the new assembly which has just been elected, Catholics are very much over-represented: 'although they comprise only nine per cent of South Vietnam's 15,300,000 people, they will hold at least twenty-six per cent of the assembly's seats'.[1] The *Catholic Herald* does not see this as an unmixed blessing. Politically, it is a great deal more sophisticated than Cardinal Spellman. There are, of course, reasons why the Catholics are over-represented. They are a minority, and a minority in great danger from a Communist victory. Most of them are refugees from North Vietnam; whether they are regarded as an equivalent of the exiled Jews in Israel or the exiled Palestinians in Jordan does not matter. They have the tenacity and unity which exile and danger produce. It is, of course, possible to disregard their danger and their claims entirely. This is done regularly in East Europe by a great many Protestants and Jews who do not feel any more sympathy with Catholics in danger of persecution than many Catholics do for Jews or Protestants. But because of the political naïveté of a great part of the American Catholic population and a great part of the American Catholic hierarchy, policy may be too much affected by the natural sentiments of the Catholic voters, as some people think it is too much affected by the natural sentiments of American Jewish voters. It is a hard saying, but American policy must not be seriously affected by the possible wrongs of Vietnamese Catholics, and there must be no repetition of the mistake against which Mr. Nehru warned the American government of relying on this minority group, better educated, more united, better disciplined than the run-of-the-mill Vietnamese, as the essen-

[1] The reference is to the *Catholic Herald*, London, September 30, 1966.

tial ally of American power. Backing minorities of this kind turns out, as a rule, to be a poor investment.

On the other hand, it seems certain that a great many people in South Vietnam do not wish to be liberated by North Vietnam, whether they are Catholics or not. As I say elsewhere, the attempted conquest of the Mekong delta by the aggressive Tongkingese is an old story. It was an old story before either the Chinese or the Russian Revolution began. The Americans might play the rôle of the French in protecting South Vietnam from invasion from the north. (The French did not do so very successfully as the infiltration continued all during French rule.) The United States might also protect Laos and Cambodia, as the French did with rather more success, against aggression from Thailand and Tongking.

But the main possibilities of political success in South Vietnam involve making political success the first priority. This means avoidance of follies like the too lavish and too warm endorsement of Marshal Ky given by President Johnson. It involves coming down on the profiteering practised both by the possessing class in South Vietnam and by too many of the American occupiers for whom the war is good business, as it was for the equivalent groups under the French régime.

To carry out the building of an effective infrastructure would require tenacity by the American builders of the infrastructure, more political intelligence in the American higher command, and in fact a kind of concealed imperialism such as the British used openly in India. There is a good deal to be said for General Gavin's policy of building an impregnable base in South Vietnam from which the Americans cannot be expelled, but from which they should be very reluctant to emerge. Such a policy needs some hope of the creation of a viable South Vietnam state, to justify it, if not of a viable Vietnamese nation. For the only viable nation in this region might simply be a

Vietnamese nation including both North and South, and of course there is no guarantee that the South Vietnamese state will not become Communist as long as the Communists show so much more energy, relevant courage, and relevant competence. Whether the materials for a viable South Vietnam state now exist I do not know. Whether they existed and could have been used if the French had been wiser, I do not know. But I am inclined to suspect that they did and could. Whether they now exist and, if so, can be used, depends on a very thorough reconsideration by the United States of what it is trying to do, what are the limits of its power, and whether what it is aiming at can be attained by a policy that seems to be, from the outside, far too heavily concentrated on military success and to have a very naïve idea of what is meant by military success.

IV

It is probable that in the long run—say in the year 2000—whatever is happening in China will be more important than anything that is happening elsewhere at this moment. But, as Keynes said, 'In the long run, we are all dead', and there are many urgent problems facing the United States which are connected with the Chinese problem in only a rather remote fashion.

For example, it is quite easy to build up a picture of the world in which General de Gaulle is conspiring against the policy of the United States in Vietnam and therefore giving what Marxists would call 'objective' aid to the Chinese Communist government in its nefarious aims. (That we do not know what these nefarious aims are, is neither here nor there in this connexion.) It is perfectly true that General de Gaulle thinks the United States is repeating the French mistake in Vietnam. It is perfectly true that, having at great political and personal risk, liquidated far more deeply rooted French interests and far more important French claims in North Africa, he is not sympathetic to arguments directed to saving American 'face' in South-East Asia. He knows the history of the French 'Community'. The history of Algeria since its independence suggests to him that easy, quick, and final solutions are in very short supply today. But this, he thinks, is no reason for not attempting to find some kind of a solution, and no reason for attempting to find solutions which will not solve anything even in a short period of time. It is very unlikely that General de Gaulle thinks that the applause he gets in Cambodia and the good relations he has with Hanoi are political factors of first-rate importance. It is equally unlikely that his attempts to get China out of the dog-house will be paid for in lavish Chinese gratitude, much less in tangible assets. Indeed, at the moment it is impossible for anyone contemplating China to make any guesses as to the results of almost any policy towards China.

But, if as I think, General de Gaulle is playing rather a weak hand in Asia, although playing it with great skill, it does not follow that, from his point of view, he is picking up no tricks, even if they are in the lower suits. Any such argument will seem to many Americans, perhaps to most Americans, brutal, selfish, short-sighted, ungrateful. All these epithets, from the American point of view, can be applied to General de Gaulle's policy without too much injustice. But not only is the General notoriously indifferent to foreign—or, indeed, to domestic—criticism; he may think that what is legitimate abuse in America is a compliment in Paris, Peking, or Hanoi. He probably remembers Pascal's dictum, 'Truth on one side of the Pyrenees, heresy on the other'. I do not think that the rôle of General de Gaulle in Asia harms the United States very much. Indeed, if it gives a way out, if the responsibility for a settlement in Vietnam which may be open to attacks by outraged patriots can be shared, General de Gaulle may be aiding the welfare of the United States although, of course, he need not deserve any credit for doing so, and there is no reason to believe that this is one of his primary motives!

But before going on to discuss much more important aspects of General de Gaulle's policy, the reaction to it in America is significant and in some ways alarming. There is, for example, a very simple explanation which is popular in the United States. General de Gaulle was snubbed (many people think rightly snubbed) by Roosevelt and is taking his belated revenge. That he was snubbed by Roosevelt, that the French policy of Roosevelt was among FDR's greatest follies, I believe to be true. But first of all, the officials of the State Department (there are some of this school) who think that the fact that the General is revenging himself for the snubs of 1942–5 justifies the policy of the Department in those years, do not seem to notice the reverse of the argument that people who guessed so wrong and who backed so many losers in that period should preserve a discreet silence today when and if that folly is being paid for.

I do not, in fact, believe that General de Gaulle is very much animated by resentment for snubs. I think he is above such petty emotions, as he is above charity and, if you like, above gratitude. Like Goethe's Pope, *Er sieht das Kleine klein; das Grosse gross*. Former friends and former enemies have discovered this in France. General de Gaulle is, in fact, less petty in his views of persons and personal differences than Franklin D. Roosevelt notoriously was.

That does not mean that the President of the French Republic cannot be led astray by ideological judgements or by what seem to me erroneous assessments of the world situation. It is possible to see that one problem is a big one and another is a small one and yet to be wrong about the character of the big problem and wrong consequently about its solution. I think it is just to say of General de Gaulle that he has a rather archaic view of French patriotism. That was his great salvation in 1940 when he had a kind of French patriotism in its own way as simple and unshakeable as that of a high officer of the American Legion. (He had, of course, many ideas which are not normally held by high officers of the American Legion.) But the world has moved on a great deal since 1940, and perhaps General de Gaulle has not adequately allowed for that movement. But the American government and the American public must remember that he feels no obligations, not that of gratitude or of allegiance. This, I think, is ungracious, especially when it takes the form of snubbing well-meaning commemorative services recalling happier moments in Franco-American relationships, but that is all. American policy should not be based on such trivial matters nor should a threat to drink only New York champagne, and thus bring General de Gaulle to his knees, be taken too seriously.[1]

The General's conspicuous ingratitude for what the United States has done for France and his arrogance, which is one of his weapons, are facts of life that have to be regretted but not to be taken too seriously. After all, the converse of his ingratitude to the United States, which liberated France, is his willingness to forgive all the sins of Germany, which conquered France. Americans really cannot have it both ways. If they wish for the pacification and unification of Europe, rudeness to the United States may be one of the necessary minor prices for the pacification and the unification.

It is at this point that clashes between American and

[1] However popular and potent this policy may be round Schenectady, it is not likely to be much noticed or even deplored in the Élysée. And many Americans asked to drink New York champagne (an excellent fluid) instead of the French champagne to which they are accustomed, may reply as Bismarck did to William II who asked him to drink German champagne, 'I will sacrifice my life for my country, but not my stomach'.

French policy or, to be more precise, between American and Gaullist policy, are really important. I myself believe that General de Gaulle is led astray by his historical memory as many Americans are led astray by theirs. It is twenty years since the liberation of France and a great deal has happened in that time, including an immense increase in France's economic power and social well-being. Not all of this, perhaps not most of this, is due to the leadership of de Gaulle; but no matter who should be getting the credit, it is a fact to be reckoned with. And it is not always a matter of not reckoning with French recovery and not always a matter of resentment over French ingratitude. The Austrian ministers, after the Czar Nicholas I had saved the Austrian Empire in 1849, announced that they would astonish the world by their ingratitude, and they did. All countries do when it suits them, when gratitude proves too expensive materially or morally.[1]

Where I think General de Gaulle's insight and prophetic powers, which have been shown to be very great, fail him is in his inability to accept in his heart, as apart from formally, the great change in the rôle of the nation states of the type of Britain or France or Germany. A change of quantity can become a change of quality, as Hegelians say, and that change has occurred. There are only two world powers, the United States and the Soviet Union. There may be a third world power, China, in 2000. There may be a third world power sooner than that, a United Europe. But none of the old traditional nations which ruled the world as late as 1914 is now in the big

[1] I can remember a lively discussion with two young Germans in West Berlin—they came from the Rhineland—who were extremely angry with the Americans for not saving them from the Russians in 1945. I was forced to point out that the Americans and Germans had not been fighting on the same side in 1945: but that did not shake their conviction of betrayal—or produce any expressions of gratitude for having been freed from Hitler.

league at all. A French army got to Moscow in 1812. A British army got to Washington in 1814. A German army nearly got to Moscow in 1941. These feats of arms are as remote from any possible realities today as the victory of Rain-in-Face over General Custer at the Little Bighorn in 1876.

This is one of the reasons why General de Gaulle, although right in this simple world in assuming that states act in their own interests and not on their alleged principles, I think misunderstands the nature of the interests of the Soviet Union. Thus when he talks of a Europe from the Channel to the Urals, he is not only by implication excluding Great Britain, regarded as an offshore island of United States territory, not as a part of Europe, but he is disregarding the fact that the term 'Russia', although it is a convenient term, is not in fact a legal title of the area of the old Russian empire; and even if it were, and the Soviet Union were nothing but the old Russian empire slightly disguised, the Russian empire has long passed the Urals. The Russians, as we are reminded, have been bullying the Chinese since the end of the seventeenth century. The Russians had territory on the North American continent as late as 1867. General de Gaulle may be willing to write off Siberia and central Asia as irrelevant possessions of the Russian state, but the Soviet Union is not willing to do so, and still less is the Chinese government, *any* Chinese government, which regards considerable parts of this territory as their rightful property, filched from the Middle Kingdom in one of its repeated periods of weakness.

However much the temperature of the cold war rises in Europe, however completely the rulers of the Soviet state have given up their hope—the basic hope of Lenin, after all—of revolutionizing the world by taking over Germany, the Soviet Union will still not be a mere European power, as France and Britain have become since the collapse of their overseas empires. The sun has most definitely set on both the French and British empires; but it has not set on the Soviet empire. It has not set on the American empire. The hostile account of the British empire written by a Bostonian-Irish poet, John Jeffrey Roche, with these famous lines:

> Her pirate flag is flying
>   Where the East and the West are one,
> And her drums when the day is dying,
>   Salute the rising sun

apply, with the deletion of the word 'pirate', to the United States even more than to the Soviet Union. This is a fact about the relations between France and the United States that nothing can alter to the advantage of France.

Then I think it is true that General de Gaulle's idea, in a phrase attributed to him falsely, of the *Europe des patries* (more properly, *Europe des gouvernements*) is open to the charges of built-in weakness rightly brought against the Articles of Confederation of 1781. The 'general welfare' of Europe in a world of great states cannot be effected and pursued by governments so loosely linked as General de Gaulle wishes them to be or made economically adequate by *ad hoc* arrangements. The most effective weapon against General de Gaulle, if the State Department thinks it is desirable to have one, is to encourage European economic integration. It is not only that out of such economic integration it is possible that a necessary political integration will come, a view of some Europeans which I used to share, but of which I am not so convinced today, but that if economic integration comes, the resulting great corporations will themselves be great powers which may have their own foreign policy and practice, including a foreign policy of close alliance with the corresponding powers inside the United States. A triple alliance of Du Pont de Nemours, Imperial Chemicals, F.G. Farben, and Rhône-Poulenc is not beyond the bounds of possibility and would present political problems which a mere *Europe des gouvernements* could not deal with.

The problems are already with Britain; they are already with France. Tariffs, quotas, complete prohibitions may save, in a kind of way, a machine-tool industry in Britain and, less certainly, in France. But machine-tool industries on this level are not likely to be effective competitors with their American super-rivals. Just as Napoleon understood very imperfectly the basis of the British economic strength which finally defeated him, so I think does General de Gaulle misunderstand the basis of American economic strength and overwhelming imperial economic power. In a sense, the United States is pursuing not the will-o'-the-wisp, but a practical policy of an economically integrated Europe which will be producing a rival for itself. Indeed, if its policy *is* to succeed, 'Europe' must be an economic rival to itself, and some of the consequences will be annoying. For example, any economic policy for the Europe of the Six must be based on a policy which will hurt American agricultural exports. A preferential market is the French price for giving up industrial protection 'inside Europe'. Again, the United States will have to do some political bookkeeping not all of whose results will be gratifying. In these ways I think General de Gaulle is swimming against the tide, and unlike Mao Tse-tung he will not, I think, be able in the long run to do this. At any rate, his successors will be unable to do this.

But having made these very serious criticisms of Gaullist policy, I should like to turn to another aspect of the Gaullist policy or Gaullist attitude to which I am not nearly as hostile or, to put it more accurately, which I accept as a fact of life with a good deal less resistance. First of all, most European countries contain a large number of people who would like their governments to 'stand up to the Yankees'. The only head of a state in Europe who dares to do so is General de Gaulle, and so far he has done so with conspicuous success. His mere existence as the head of the French state was a defeat of American policy at the very height of American power, that is to say in the last years of the last war. This is noticed inside and outside France. There are millions of thwarted Gaullists not only in Germany, where they are vocal and numerous, but in Britain, where they are numerous but not quite so vocal. The same kind of nationalist passion which produced anti-American dictatorships in Latin America, and has done so for many years, has produced them in roughly relevant circumstances in Europe. I regret this, but again it is a fact that the American public and the American government will have to reckon with. It is not merely a question of 'do a man a good turn, and he will never forgive you', although that is an important element, but it is a question of an unconscious American assumption that any serious difference with the United States is wrong, foolish, and destined to failure. Few Europeans in their heart of hearts accept this simple identification of political virtue with an automatic support of American policy. To go back to an historical parallel, weak European countries object to being treated as were the 'allies of the Roman people' under the Roman Empire.

I myself think that the United States, given all its temptations and given all its temporary monopoly of power, behaved with magnanimity and wisdom. Not all its agencies showed these qualities, but that is a human weakness not confined to agents of the United States. But it is an important truth to remember that General de Gaulle is speaking for far more people than he claims to speak for, and that far more people object to his manner than object to his matter. 'If this be treason, make the most of it'.

It is of course possible that not only General de Gaulle but the rulers of Britain and Germany are making a dangerous bet which may turn out to be disastrous. Perhaps the situation which fully justified the creation of

NATO and the buttressing up of Europe against another *coup* like that of Prague can recur. Perhaps some unpredictable flurry of Soviet policy may revive the dangers of 1948, and then we shall all be sorry that some of the defences assembled then have been dismantled. That a man whose judgement I admire as much as I do that of Mr. Dean Acheson feels this as a very real danger impresses me. But I am also impressed by the fact that it is as difficult to keep the old NATO together as it has proved for the Soviet Union to keep its imperial control intact. The Holy Alliance, to go back to a not totally irrelevant historical parallel, had lost its virtue within fifteen years of its foundation; NATO after all has had a longer life than that, and a much longer life than the coalition against Germany in the First War or against Hitler in the Second. But in its old character, it cannot, for good or ill, survive much longer. It might have died of anaemia even if it had not been bludgeoned by General de Gaulle. From this possibly depressing state of affairs, American policy must start.

In the rest of the world, it has not been a case of running very fast to stand still. Four-fifths of the human race have run very fast and have not stood still, but have gone backwards. In Asia and in Latin America, great and overwhelming problems which puzzled the most enlightened leaders still puzzle less enlightened or less potent successors. There can be no doubt that many of the hopes based on the new African states ten years ago have proved to be baseless, and a possible crack-up of Nigeria after a series of *coups* and counter-*coups* is perhaps the most important and the most depressing fact of African history today. Some of the confidence with which South Africa, Southern Rhodesia and Portugal face the disapproving outer world comes from the destruction of the hopes put in the new resurgent Africa in which it has proved, alas, much easier to destroy than to build up. There are bright patches in Latin America, but they are only bright patches. Neither the state of Brazil nor the state of Argentina is at the moment likely to encourage hopes of the rapid and visible progress envisaged by President Kennedy. This is a depressing balance sheet, and contemplating it frankly may anger as well as depress an optimistic people like the Americans. But nothing can absolve them from the risks and privileges and duties of being the most powerful nation of the 'free world' or, more shortly still, the most powerful nation of the world. To land a man on the moon and fail to solve the problems of Bolivia and Mississippi will be a very ironical comment on the triumphs of technology!

There is not much for comfort in the present American situation; there is not much for comfort in the present European situation. But even in Britain, the troubles are minor compared with those facing Africa, Asia, and South America. The American people and government will be called on to digest, at the very height of their confidence and power, the wisdom of the old Italian shoeblack on Wall Street who was asked what he had learned after forty years' work in 'the street'. He replied, 'I have learned that there is no free lunch'. The power, the safety, even the ability to change the world for the better, has a very high price now, as it always has had, and it would be wise if the American people learned to allow for the price in the policies they and their government adopt.

I

'THE Past is Prologue'. More than one American scholar in recent years has recalled this truth to the American people, for a great many American academics—and others—are and have been for a long time alarmed at the shortness of the historical view of the average American. They are afraid, as Santayana said, that those who know nothing of the past are fated to repeat it; and they know that a great deal of the past casts light, and necessary light, on the present. Few people who reflect on the state of the American public mind (or perhaps on the public mind of any democratic society) can doubt the truth of the Shakespearian dictum and the importance of its general acceptance.

Perhaps at the present moment (the spring of 1965) it is most important to insist on the fact that 'the past is present'. It is a dangerous foreshortening to see the past merely as a prologue and whatever is happening at this moment as an act, perhaps a last act, in world history and an act moving to a distinct end of good and evil.

There is, of course, a great deal to be said in practical life for the American indifference to a great many ancient historical problems. The absence in the American consciousness of these remote historical problems is a great advantage. This is made more evident when we consider that one great historical problem is, in fact, present today in the United States, the race problem, and its presence is one of the handicaps and one of the agonies of American life in this century. But since the United States is now deeply involved with the outside world, the belief that, to quote from Bishop Berkeley,

Westward the course of empire takes its way;
  The four first acts already past,
A fifth shall close the drama with the day:
  Time's noblest offspring is the last

can be dangerous. It is very unlikely that the American people can, in fact, live in the last act of history, unless it is to come to a very sudden end, and soon, and not certain that 'time's noblest offspring is the last'.[1]

What do I mean, that the past is present and not merely prologue? It is present because a great many historical problems posed by 'Nature', by 'God', by 'the Dialectic', by 'original sin', by 'the time spirit', by whatever words one chooses to use to explain the present perplexities and dangers, are still with us with as much intensity and power of mischief as when they first came on the historical scene 200 or 2,000 years ago. That the American citizen, the American taxpayer, the American soldier should be faced with expensive and dangerous problems today because of mistakes made or quarrels started in what is, by American standards, a very remote past, is a hard saying. But it is a hard saying that needs saying today. To give an instance, to which I shall have to return: the rulers of China in its first great expansionist period began to interfere in what we call Indo-China or Vietnam about the time that Caesar invaded Britain; but the results of the Chinese intervention have been continuous in a way that Roman intervention has not been. We are not forced to think back to the remote and mythical world of King Lear or of Cymbeline or even

[1] It was because of this great Irish philosopher's prophetic sense of the importance of North America that the founders of the University of California chose Berkeley as the name of the college town in which they planted the new university and inscribed the famous quatrain over the entrance gate. Recent events (after the giving of these lectures) have shown that both the Regents of the University and Bishop Berkeley were a little optimistic in thinking that the last and beneficent act of history had begun!

to the comparatively peaceful history of the Roman province of Britain. The ebb and flow of China's relations with its southern neighbours have never ceased since that remote time. That is a thing to remember in face of the problems of South-East Asia today.

But before I turn, as I shall do later, to contemporary problems, there are certain basic reflexions I should like to put before you. First of all, it is quite natural that Americans in North America or, indeed, in South America should feel remote from the Asiatic or the European past. From the point of view of the white settlers in North America, at any rate north of Mexico, they brought their history with them and brought comparatively little of it. The Negroes who were forcibly imported were stripped of their history by the slavery system. The Indians' social, religious, economic life was profoundly altered by the impact of the white invaders and their history is a romantic part of the American legend, but not in a serious sense part of American life. This, of course, is in many ways a great advantage for the American people, as I have already suggested. People who quote Goethe's famous poem beginning *Amerika, du hast es besser*, often forget what he thought the Americans *had* better. And what the Americans had better was simply the absence of the historical burdens that lay so heavily on the European peoples. These provided admirable raw materials for literary effort, as Goethe himself showed in his own writing, but were far from being a political asset in the modern world. And, whether consciously or not, the American people treat history as 'usable', to be taken up, used, discarded like a new plastic container.

This may seem paradoxical in a country which has more professional historians than perhaps the whole of the rest of the world put together, which studies its own history and the history of the outside world with unprecedented learning, which preserves relics of very varying merit of the remote and in many ways irrelevant Indian past; but it is one thing for Henry Ford to reconstruct Dearborn Village or for the Rockefellers to rebuild (some would say create) Williamsburg and for Americans to think seriously that contemporary problems and policies are to be assessed in terms set by people dead for hundreds of years, still less by peoples destroyed centuries ago. Henry Ford paying for the building of Dearborn Village, reconstructing the school house to which Mary brought her little lamb, and Henry Ford saying 'History is bunk' are not contrasting and opposing figures; they are the same figure and a very American figure. History is for Ford, and for many Americans, a source of family pride and social comfort, of amusement, but it is not something that commands and organizes present experience. Alas, for a great part of the world, history is commanding, is organizing, and for those parts of the primitive world in which this is still not true, progress is rapidly providing history, sometimes fictitious, for the emergent nation states whose mere existence is the result not only of history in the sense of what has happened in the past, but of what Europeans, Chinese and others have said about that past.

What are relevant considerations for an American statesman or an American citizen facing the world today to have before his mind? First of all, he must accept the fact that his own situation is anomalous and highly privileged. The Mexicans, the Peruvians cannot get away from the great Aztec and the great Inca past. As relics of the Spanish Empire, they cannot get away from the Castilian past. As children of Europe, they cannot get away from the European past. Of course, the American people, that is, the people of the United States, cannot get away from the European past either and cannot get away from their own past. But so far, their history has been so fortunate, their self-confidence so complete that they suffer less from historical burdens than any other country except possibly Australia and New Zealand. And Australia and New Zealand know this, though they would admit that they are not free from other peoples' history since they are in fact vulnerable and exposed to masses of population with very old histories—one is tempted to say with far too much history.

One result of the unique character of the North American experience is that 'isolationism' is natural, and has been for long periods of time practicable, and is even today, if not something that can be attained, something that can be sighed for nostalgically. The most one can say to the American who laments the days when isolation was a fact, and isolationism less a fact than a mere description of that fact, is ' "Nice work if you can get it", but you can't get it'.

One of the discoveries of historical research in this century has been the great extension of our notion of what we mean by 'civilization'. Europeans and descendants of Europeans naturally fall into thinking of the world as Europe, and by Europe we mean in practice, roughly speaking, the Roman Empire. When we learn that the Roman Emperor ordered the whole world to be enrolled and this led to the journey to Bethlehem, we must remember that the 'whole world' was the world of the Mediterranean basin, north and south of the sea, and just beginning to extend into northern Europe. Yet at that time, Chinese civilization was already much older, more complicated in many ways, more sophisticated, and at least as impressive as the Greco-Roman civilization of the *oecumene*, the *orbis terrarum*, as the Greeks and Romans saw the Mediterranean basin which had been made one by the combination of Greek ideas and Roman military power and law.

Until well into the nineteenth century, 'the World' was the European world and the New World was America, the child of the old. This produced a great deal of natural but absurd arrogance that was passed on to the European immigrants who settled in the Americas, above all to the

English immigrants who settled in what is now the United States. Part of this arrogance was due to the increasing intolerance of Christian attitudes to 'pagans'. The famous line from the 'Chanson de Roland', *les païens ont tort* (the heathen are wrong), described an attitude that prevailed long after the eleventh century; and even today we find it strange and irritating that the heathen do not admit that they are wrong and do not even admit that they are heathen, pagans or inferiors. After all, 'pagan' in late Latin merely means hicks, country folk, and hicks have been in the strictest sense of the term the vast majority of the human race since organized human society first appeared. It was silly and unChristian for the late Hilaire Belloc to say that 'Europe is the Faith and the Faith is Europe'; but it was not as silly or as unChristian when he said it forty years ago as it would be today when the weight of the exterior pagan world is beginning to be heavily felt.

But we now know, ignoring moral questions of arrogance and religious intolerance or lack of charity, that in fact neither the Romans nor the Greeks thought they were alone in the world or that the *orbis terrarum*, the *oecumene* was all that mattered. For the Greeks, all non-Hellenes (including the Romans) were barbarians, and the only universal order the Romans recognized was that of being citizens of no mean city, that is, being Roman citizens, a term which lost all local meaning. But we now know that the Greeks and the Romans knew much more about the outside world than we used to think, knew more about Africa, knew more about Asia, had more dealings, commercial, military, intellectual, with their Asiatic and African neighbours than we used to believe.

It is a long time now since Professor Teggart of California called our attention to the appearance, at roughly the same time, of figures like Buddha, Socrates, and the later Hebrew prophets. The traces of the empire of Alexander can be found in place names to this day as far east as India. And we know, in reverse, that upheavals in central Asia, caused possibly by desiccation or by other changes of climate or by tribal feuds of whose origins we know nothing, sent tremors to the Atlantic shores. We know the Romans had trading ports as far east as Burma, that a deficient balance of trade with China was one of the economic troubles of the later Roman Empire, that for Europe China was the link with Japan, and that across the Sahara traders went north and south from Roman Africa to what we now call black Africa. I could multiply instances of the intermingling of trade, politics, war which make the old impression of automatic European isolation or superiority nonsense. And for the many Europeans and the many Americans who share this old traditional feeling of superiority, a little study of American historical research in these fields of cultural and economic changes would be a very good political investment!

Of course it is quite a long time now since the automatic superiority over the heathen, who 'in his blindness bows down to wood and stone', was replaced by an almost excessive veneration for Eastern wisdom. Reading the diaries and letters of New England Transcendentalists of the early nineteenth century, one would get the impression, almost totally false, that study of the *Bhagavad-Gita* had replaced the study of the Gospels, or that the Vedic hymns had replaced the hymns of Wesley! But the notion of a world in which nearly all people outside the Americas were, if not united, in constant, often fruitful contact, was one of the great discoveries of the nineteenth century very much reinforced by the greatly improved research techniques of the twentieth.[1] For it makes plain to us, or should

[1] To ward off possible attacks by zealous Italians, I can only say I do not think that Viking settlements in North America, wherever they were (and in all probability there were some) are part of the American usable past or that North America entered 'world history', in the sense in which I am using the term, before Columbus. The deeds of the

make plain to us, that there can be no justification for a view of history which sees it culminating, necessarily and finally, in North Atlantic civilization, in the achievements of Europe and of its gigantic child America (by which I mean here the United States, if Canadians and Mexicans and others will forgive me).

But apart from improving our manners towards what Kipling called 'the lesser breeds without the law', what is the utility of such reflexions? They have, I think, a very great utility today, and especially in the United States. For it was natural that in the heyday of European and American self-admiration, the heyday of belief that the fifth act of history was opening and was necessarily the noblest, we should believe that the agenda of history would be determined by us in terms of our own past and present, of our own needs and ideals. I say 'us', for until at any rate the Second World War many people in Europe, not shaken out of their complacency by the First World War, still believed that Europe was the leader, if no longer the automatic, dominant leader, in the North Atlantic civilization, and that the North Atlantic civilization was destined, one almost says by divine right, to determine the present and the future of the human race.

In a sense, it was easy enough to accept the fact that there was a great deal of history, before Columbus discovered the islands of the Caribbean or before Vasco da Gama sailed to India. But with this unification of the whole world (if we forget for a moment the long delay in discovering Australia), prehistory ended and real history began. And by real history we have all tended to mean what I would call 'white' history.

Few Europeans, few Americans, however much they admire the picturesque aspects of Asiatic or African cul-

Vikings were heroic but they were isolated. And Australia and New Zealand were of course even more isolated from the great mass of mankind.

ture or the commercial utility of Asiatic and African resources, including slaves, thought of them as serious rivals for the rightful domination of mankind. Intelligent Jesuit missionaries could admire the sophisticated civilization of India, of China and of Japan. But already the quite recent military and naval superiority of the white peoples was breeding delusions of grandeur from which we have not yet escaped. Even in the eighteenth century, when admiration for China was part of the creed of the *philosophes*, the men of the 'Enlightenment', of whom the two most eminent American specimens were Benjamin Franklin and Thomas Jefferson, few realized that the great Manchu emperors of China were the richest in everything except modern military forces, the most powerful and, possibly, the wisest rulers in the world. Going to India in a 'time of troubles' such as the sub-continent had, like China, often known, enabled a handful of British merchants to become imperial rulers and, what was possibly only an historical accident, a temporary breakdown in Indian political resources allowed the creation of that astonishing anomaly, the British Indian Empire. The quite recent superiority of the West in political unification, in arms, in the militarily important types of metallurgy, was added to the old Christian feeling of being theologically right, and to the much more modern feeling bred by the Renaissance, by the scientific revolution, and by the new ideas of the eighteenth century, that the Europeans and the Europeans alone understood the nature of things. And from this natural if unfortunate sense of superiority and the refusal to reflect that the superiority might be accidental and might be temporary, sprang a number of habits of mind which are great hindrances today both to the much weakened European powers and to the immensely strengthened American power.

It is painful for us to reflect that past historical achievements of which we know nothing, that past historical quarrels which are nothing to us, that past religious and philosophical beliefs which mean little or nothing to us, are yet part of our business today. But the time is passed when one could, like Macaulay, confidently hope to turn the Indians into 'brown Englishmen'. That the offering of the resources of European culture and science to the backward peoples would be accepted, but not on the terms on which it was offered; that in India our own historical past was part of our present, but that the historical past of these remote, little-known, and at this time generally despised people, was part of our present too—this was hard to swallow. And this innocent sense of superiority and this innocent assumption of the irrelevance of the past experience of the greater part of the human population came most naturally to the Americans settling in the great, empty, and immensely rich continent of North America where they *could* cast off a great part and the most hampering part of their European inheritance and assume that the only necessary dealing with the inheritors of the rest of the world was to teach them how to imitate as best they could the American way of life.

I should like to emphasize that this attitude, dangerous, possibly disastrous, as it is, was not, of course, invented by Americans and is not even today confined to them. There is a deep truth in the dictum of Thomas Sancton that 'every white man is at heart a sahib'. One can still read with astonishment of the complacent sense of moral and religious superiority with which the Portuguese approached India and China, with which the Dutch approached what we now call Indonesia, with which the Spaniards approached Mexico and Peru. The hangover of this attitude, more and more intolerable to the great majority of the world's peoples, is one of the handicaps to be offset against the technological and military superiority of the whites. A sense of military and technical superiority is most manifest in America; yet an attitude of superiority in Americans is more damaging than an attitude of superiority in the citizens of the decaying or decayed imperial powers like Britain and France. For the resentment of this attitude is directed for the most part against the United States. This is a response to American power, not to any special dose of original sin in the Americans.

Dr. Johnson once gave the wise but uncomfortable advice: 'Clear your mind of cant'. He did not mind people talking cant: what he objected to, was people believing in their own cant. And one of the handicaps of our inherited notions of superiority is that we not only talk cant, we believe it. And the world, naturally enough, does not believe our cant and resents our apparent simple faith in it, as an insult added to already very grave injury.

What do I mean in this context by cant? First of all, there is the assumption, not argued but assumed to be proved by historical experience, that the superiority of the West and the whites is a given fact of history and an unalterable fact of history. Indeed, history begins for a great many Americans with the assertion of this superiority. An assertion of superiority, it must be noticed, is not the same thing as an assertion of difference. It would be very foolish to fall back on some of the optimistic illusions of the late nineteenth century in which all cultural, political, religious, technical differences were seen as minor obstacles to the creation of a unified world culture in which the African on his bicycle in Bulawayo was much the same as the London shop boy on his bicycle in, say, Wimbledon. This was the illusion which H. G. Wells first shared and then discarded.

It would be absurd to say that this illusion has been discarded by everybody, for a good deal of our approach, and even of the American approach, to the outside world is based on the belief that the vast majority of the human race can and should and will become the equivalent of Macaulay's 'brown Englishmen', although for America they will be 'brown Americans'. Even in the United States, the assumption is that all the very divergent strains which make up the American population can be fused by a process of 'Americanization' which will produce, roughly speaking, a new type of population with the basic ideas that come from the historical experience of the original Protestant settlers in North America, the 'ethnic' group that we now call WASPS, a new American type, but the result of the adjustment of the new immigrant stocks to the old American type. The Americanization programme may, of course, make a little play with the cultural contributions of the newcomers, like certain types of cookery, certain types of folk art, notably of jazz, the great contribution, from this point of view, of the American negro; but, basically, Americanization means stripping a good part of the American population of its own inherited culture.

It should be said, first of all, that there is a good deal of sense in this, that it is highly desirable in a nation, to quote from President Kennedy, 'a nation of immigrants', to provide a common culture and it has been one of the great functions and one of the great successes of the American education system to provide this culture, to make what are, historically speaking, artificial traditions accepted as if they were inherited from a fairly remote antiquity and part of the spontaneous reactions of all Americans.

Nevertheless even inside the United States, the Negro problem shows in the most dramatic form that it is not easy to create a real national culture if the inherited elements of the culture of a great part of the population are disregarded entirely or classified as of minor importance. I do not think (I am glad to report) that the attempt to make all the various racial strains in America united in a new homogeneous type will succeed, and it is certainly not pursued with the same naïve assumption of virtue as marked, for example, the Americanization campaigns that followed the

First World War, of which the Ku-Klux-Klan was an odious parody! But the worst of that coercive Americanization seems to be over and out of the extremely fluid American society today a new and genuinely 'American' type may be emerging, a culture of the future, not a culture of an arbitrarily selected past. Anyway, that is a problem of American internal policy and of importance here only so far as the attitude behind the old Americanization policy is reflected outside the United States.

Unfortunately, it is being reflected. For a great deal of American propaganda abroad and a great deal of American political and social action abroad is innocently imperialist in the sense that it does expect the world to turn American and sees too many problems in simple terms of adopting or imitating the American 'way of life'.

To avoid approaching the outer world with this attitude is extremely difficult for Americans, since they have, in both religious and general terms, a strong missionary bent. I am convinced, for instance, that American interest in China, American devotion to an image of China, American disagreements with China owe far more to the century-old American missionary entanglement than to any economic or even political interests. China was to be won for Christ —for Christ interpreted in North American Protestant terms in this century. It seems pretty safe to say that this was always a faint hope, and is visibly a faint hope today. But the attitude has not died with the failure of the experiment to which the older American culture gave so much love, so much money, and so many men and women of devotion.

I do not think it is paradoxical to say that some of the illusions of the American people about China were and are illusions of the American missionaries in face of one of the great revulsions against foreign influence and foreign conquest which can be seen in Chinese history since long before the United States existed. That the American, that the European intrusion into Chinese history could seem to an educated Chinese of the old school or a Marxian Chinese of the new school a mere ripple on the surface of Chinese history, or a mere ripple in the Marxian future, is a truth very difficult indeed for Europeans, used to more than a century of Chinese impotence, to accept (and Russians are Europeans in this sense). But it is still more difficult for Americans to accept it, since their foreshortening of history allows nothing for the immense Chinese historical memory, and their pragmatical approach to history allows nothing for the Marxist conviction that the future is known. And that future is an unAmerican future.

Europeans who had missionary, financial, military and other investments in China know that their investments have been lost. It is not even remembered in America that the greatest missionary effort ever expended in China was not expended by Protestant America, but by Catholic France. Few Frenchmen now believe that that investment can be saved. The forcible opening of China to the West was the work of imperial Britain, as the later opening of Japan was the work of republican America. But no one in Britain any longer has the illusions bred by the easy successes of the First and Second Chinese Wars, by the creation of Shanghai, by the double occupations of Peking by European (and in the second instance American) troops.

Europeans with some historical knowledge can remember Christian endeavours in China which failed in the thirteenth century, can remember all the many hopes that have been formed and lost in repeated efforts to bring China into the commonwealth of Christendom. European pessimism, at the moment, is probably more helpful in dictating policy towards China than American optimism.

I have chosen China as an example of the crippling effects of a foreshortening of history in the American mind; but of course there are other examples. There is the easy belief that Russia became a potent and dangerous power affecting the United States only since the Bolshevik Revolution,[1] and it is assumed that the rôle of Russia in China has been necessarily a Marxist rôle and necessarily an aspect of the doctrinal imperialism of Communism. It has been in part a Marxist rôle, as the American rôle has been in part a Christian rôle. But Russia forced its first 'superior' treaty on Manchu China just about the time of the foundation of Pennsylvania. A great part of what the Chinese thought, and still think, natural Chinese territory was seized by Russia in the early nineteenth century, as the covered wagons were crossing the plains. Many of the present problems of Chinese and Russian relations can be understood only in terms of the inheritance by the Soviet government of the policies of the Czars and by the Chinese government, *any* Chinese government, of the policies of the Manchu emperors. These seem historical platitudes, but they are useful historical platitudes. Platitudes or not, what is their importance today?

The first platitude whose importance must be understood is that many problems arise in the world and are arising today, notably in Asia, with which the United States had in the past nothing to do, may have not very much to do today, and may have nothing to do in the not very remote future. There may be a real clash along the 2,000-mile frontier between the Soviet Union and Communist China or, to make my point more effectively, between Russia and China. But that clash has little to do with any of the grounds of quarrel between Russia and the United States and the United States and China.

I do not deny for a moment the missionary zeal of Communism: it adds a new ingredient to the witches' brew. But the witches were busy with the brew, again long before

[1] I remember being asked at a conference about twelve years ago why Roosevelt at Yalta had allowed Russia to become a Pacific power. I could only reply that Russia had been a Pacific power before the United States existed.

the United States existed. It is important, that is to say, to avoid the easy assumption that historical problems only come into existence, or only become important, when they in some way or another impinge on the interests or sentiments or economic or military needs of the United States. There are many problems in the world which the American people didn't create and cannot solve. This is not to say that some of these problems are not problems in which the American people need not take a great and intelligent interest, and in which their government need not be involved; but they are not simple problems to be solved in naïve American terms.

Consequently, in the day-to-day aspects of politics, in the internal and obscure in-fighting of international Communist leadership, in the leaders' policies which arise from natural catastrophes like drought and famine, earthquake and flood, the United States simply cannot be a spectator. It may not be able to prevent the drought or flood or undo the damage of either. Communist China might well have suffered more, not only from the follies of its government during the period of the 'Great Leap Forward', but from a temporarily hostile Nature, and recent good harvests in China may undo the result of the follies of the Chinese government, whatever America does about China in a hostile or a tolerant spirit.[1]

It is not only in China, which naturally preoccupies the

[1] At the time I gave these lectures, I had not foreseen the degree to which Chinese leadership in 1964 would make a series of mistakes of which possibly the most important in the long run will prove to be the intensification of the power struggle *inside* the Communist world, the pushing of the ideological war against Russia to extremes; and, possibly less important, but still very important, the overplaying of the Communist hand in Indonesia, which may cause a revulsion from China based less on ideological or moral scruples, than on the fact that a great part of the population of Asia, a great part of the population of the whole world, likes to back a winner. And at the moment China does not look like being a winner.

public mind, that these truths are relevant. If one considers the great world problems today as being reducible in black and white terms to an 'irrepressible conflict' between the 'free world' and the 'Communist world', one may of course be right in the long run or in the not very long run. But in the quite short run, the American government and the American people may be making a series of expensive mistakes by seeing everything that happens in the world in the light of this conflict, as possibly the *early* Crusaders saw the whole political problems of the Mediterranean basin in terms of a Holy War against the *paynim*. (The Crusaders, it must be remembered, soon got over this naïve idea, and the Crusades became less and less Crusades and more and more rackets.)

For instance, if we accept without examination the concept 'free world', it must seem obvious that all the minor conflicts, however interesting or irritating or ancient, should give way to the necessities of this final struggle of Good against Evil. In war, we assume, very optimistically, that allies will make every kind of sacrifice for the common victory, even abandoning old loyalties and old enmities in pursuit of this common end. No alliance that I know of has ever attained this height of unselfish unity. That most successful alliance, between France and the new United States in 1778, was threatened throughout its existence by the very different interests, in detail if not in the mass, of the King of France and the American people. It is hardly necessary to recall the victorious alliances of the First and Second World Wars, to remind ourselves of the difficulties of waging what used to be called 'Coalition' war; and these difficulties would have been very great even if the Soviet Union in the Second War had been a candid, loyal, and unideological partner. The clashes between President Roosevelt, Prime Minister Churchill, General de Gaulle are proof enough of how three men, with one common object, each with a high degree of responsibility, could have a very different set of priorities, and very different views on ways and even, in detail, on means.

It is idle, therefore, to expect that the peoples of the world will see their immediate problems in terms that suit the policies of the United States, either by being so obviously right that the United States can back them in the common cause without hesitation, or so obviously wrong that they are almost as much enemies as the Soviet Union and Communist China are.

The world is not as simple as that. For example, it may still seem to the American people—as indeed it does to me—that the common interests of India and Pakistan in immunity from Russian and Chinese joint or several pressure should be paramount. The late John Foster Dulles was angered by the refusal of India 'to stand up and be counted', to use a revealing American phrase with its overtones of religious conversion as well as of democratic politics. But it seems obvious to me that he took Pakistan's devotion to the cause of the 'free world' much too seriously. For Pakistan had, its rulers thought, in the Kashmir question a more urgent problem to solve than the problems that so perplexed and angered and worried the American Secretary of State. This may have been, and may still be, a sign of very bad judgement on the part of the rulers of Pakistan. But that is the situation with which the American government is faced and to which there is no adequate black and white solution.[1]

Trying in good faith to build up states able to resist the separate or concurrent pressure of Russia and China, the United States has found itself hampered, perhaps fatally hampered, in this aim, by a shabby bargain made by the British East India Company over a century ago, after the destruction of the Sikh state, a bargain which resulted in

[1] This lecture was given before the friction between India and Pakistan over Kashmir, dating from 1947, broke out in 1965 in open war.

the creation of the absurd and historically rootless state of Kashmir. It is hard that the American people and the American government should have to pay for shabby bargains made by British rulers and Hindu adventurers over a century ago; but this is a hard world.

In the same way, a rational Vietnam policy for the United States is made even more difficult than it would be in any event by a series of historical deals, attacks and withdrawals, treaties and private agreements made by the states and by the imperial powers in South-East Asia when America was, in both theory and practice, profoundly isolationist. For example, one of the problems facing any power in dealing with what used to be called French Indo-China is that the French interrupted what one might call the natural imperialism of the rulers of North Vietnam, or the empire of Annam, or of the militant, industrious, aggressive, and brave Tongkingese. In all probability, but for the French intervention and the conquest of what they called Indo-China, there would have been a unified Indo-China under *some* native power based on the north, or possibly based on the north with Chinese support.

After all, the French had to fight a naval war with China and even a minor land war to cut off Chinese support from Tongkingese resistance to French imperialism during the first presidency of Grover Cleveland. Many of the troubles that are facing the United States today over the boundaries of and policy on Laos and Cambodia, over the rôle of the *montagnards*, date from French rule—from its successes as well as from its failures. If Thailand exists as the only non-colonized country in South-East Asia, this is less due to its own powers of resistance or to French moderation than to the fact that the British government wished to keep Thailand, or, as it was then called, Siam, as a buffer state between its own recently conquered colony of Burma and the French recently conquered colony of Annam. I could multiply the instances in which the United States is faced with very unsatisfactory adjustments often effected two generations ago, by problems of power blocks in Europe as much as by political questions or ambitions in South-East Asia.

Less urgent, but not unimportant as an example of the possibly depressing truth that the past is present is the state of Africa. For when we talk of 'Ghana', 'Nigeria', 'Sierra Leone', the 'Côte d'Ivoire', 'Senegal', we are talking not of creations of African history or even of African power, but of creations of European power and of European diplomacy. The Congo, which has been the main headache in Africa since the end of the last war, is an extremely artificial creation of international diplomacy and as much a result of the hopes and fears of Bismarck about the balance of power in Europe, as of the greed of such spreaders of civilization as King Leopold II of the Belgians. This history—not, in fact, very ancient, and not very creditable—is still with us, and still with the American people. It will not help American policy very much to remember the details of the frontiers established at the Berlin Congress of 1884 or of minor deals that produced such anomalies as the 'Caprivi Strip' on the edge of the Rhodesias. But the fact that the African state structure is of European creation and may not long survive in the way that the Europeans planned it, even under independent native governments, is another hard saying which ought to be listened to.

Again, it is not enough to talk of the 'nationality' of Ghana, of the Congo, without reflecting in what ways this nationality resembles or does not resemble the nationality, let us say, of Britain or France, of Ireland or of Italy.

Even in Latin America, which in many ways is like North America, there can be a great deal of the *damnosa hereditas* of the ancient world. Many frontiers, many barriers to the rational utilization of water power, mineral resources, oil resources, harbours date either from decisions made by Spanish viceroys or from the accidents of the wars of liberation. The American diplomatist who rashly said that Bolivia had no reason for existing was tactless, but he was saying something which is not quite nonsense and is not quite impertinence. Bolivia, Paraguay have suffered a great deal in this century from wars over frontiers which seem even more irrational, even more self-destroying than wars over frontiers in Europe; and the United States has had nothing to do in the past with the conditions that produced the Paraguayan wars of the nineteenth and twentieth centuries. As I have said elsewhere, it is fortunate that there are very few Paraguayans as they are possibly the most militant and effectively militant people in the world! North Americans did not always think so; but it is a fact about Paraguay that we have got to realize.

There are very few places in the world outside the Arctic and Antarctic continents where this history is not present, where it is not very unmanageable, where it does not run counter to natural American prepossessions and principles. It is natural for the Americans to dream of a paradise lost or a paradise mislaid in which these things did not matter. There was a brief period in the nineteenth century (brief as the scale of world history goes) when Americans *could* ignore all these things or be intensely optimistic about their own impact on the exterior world and their power to educate or lead the world in exclusively American terms. But not later than the Second World War, and I should say not later than the First World War, the angel with the fiery sword expelled the American Adam and, politically even more serious, the American Eve from the Garden of Eden. And a great deal of American troubles today seem to me to come from the nostalgia for an Eden whose gates have been closed for ever, not mainly through the sins of the American Adam and Eve, but the sins of continents that have an older, less cheerful, but alas still highly relevant history.

II

It is one of the great difficulties of the study of comparative politics and of the study of foreign relations, that the student finds it difficult to free himself from habits of thought that were rational and plausible, if incorrect, when he formed them, but are now irrelevant and hurtful.

I am, for instance, old enough to remember, since I was a precocious little boy, the world before 1914, and am quite convinced that many of my automatic reactions and judgements date from that time although they are totally irrelevant, or nearly totally irrelevant, to the world of 1965. For example, I can remember the establishment of a parliamentary constitution in Turkey and in Persia, as it was then called; and I can remember being, for some obscure reason, a partisan of the Russian Liberal Party. I was optimistic about the results of the Chinese revolution of 1912, and on learning that an eminent Scottish scholar had gone to China to act as political adviser to the new government, I was puzzled, since it seemed to me quite simple to be political adviser to China now that they had got rid of the Manchus and all such old abuses as foot-binding. The thing to do was to adopt the British constitution. From that time, progress could automatically be made.

I have lost most of these illusions today. But I fear that a great many people of my own age or older have not lost them. I feel, for example, that the late John Foster Dulles preserved into his old age as Secretary of State, some of the illusions quite natural when he was secretary to his grandfather, John Foster, who was Secretary of State, and worked with his uncle, Robert Lansing, who was also Secretary of State. Yet the illusions of a little boy like myself, and the illusions of a young man like John Foster Dulles were not imbecile illusions before 1914. Because the technical superiority which the West had suddenly revealed in the eighteenth and early nineteenth centuries made it easy, indeed almost inevitable, to believe that the future of the world would be determined by the white world, by what we now call the North Atlantic Community, so united in spirit and, as most people thought, united in a causal relationship with the natural superiority of the Western world.

It was a very widespread belief that it was because Britain was the most politically advanced state in Europe, i.e. the most liberal state in Europe, that it took the lead in the eighteenth century over France which had more natural endowments. It was believed that 'free institutions', *habeas corpus*, parliament, public controls, a fairly free press, did not merely occur at the same time and in the same country as the invention of the first economically useful steam engine, but were parts of the same process. The steam engine was invented in the country which had a free press.

There was some justification for this belief. First of all, the English revolution of the seventeenth century, the *real* revolution, the execution of Charles I, the establishment of the Commonwealth, the destruction of the relics of English legal feudalism—did give England, and after 1707 Scotland, a head start. The middle classes flourished in what was, by the standards of the time, an 'open society'. True, what was left of feudalism in France was merely an archaic nuisance, but it was a nuisance. True, the elaborate guild system and the elaborate regulation of commerce and manufacture by the French government were under greater and greater strain, but they still existed. Some relics of the medieval order still existed even in Britain. To use a famous example, the young James Watt when trying to improve the existing and uneconomic steam engines of the time ran athwart, in my native city of Glasgow, the rights of the Glasgow guilds. As he was not a 'Hammerman', he had no right to be tinkering with any kind of machinery. But he was allowed to go on doing so because Professor Adam Smith got him a job in the University, and the medieval privileges of the University protected him against the medieval privileges of the Hammermen. James Watt found it convenient to leave his native land for England and to settle in Birmingham which, unlike Glasgow, was not an incorporated city or, as we say in Scotland, a Royal Burgh, but an unorganized village which had the great advantage of having no privileges for anybody. And it is not impossible that the fact that James Watt was later accused of being a 'Jacobin'—as bad then as being accused of being a Communist today—came from his adoption of the view that the old order required basic transformations to make way for the new order and the new industry in which he was a leader.

I think there is no doubt that the prestige of English parliamentary government, which was very great after the fall of Napoleon, owed a great deal of its power to the visible fact that only the new industry had permitted England to resist Napoleon. The old mercantile and agricultural England of the eighteenth century, although very rich by the standards of that age, could not have withstood the French Empire. The new industrial England could and did.

At any rate, it was the almost universal belief of the believers in progress (there were a good many intelligent people who had doubts about the value of progress, e.g. Coleridge), that there was a causal relationship between 'freedom' and 'progress'. The economic backwardness of a great part of Europe was attributed to its political backwardness, and I think there is some truth in this, and that France did suffer (and Germany suffered still more) from political obstacles to economic expansion. And it was noted that the first European country to become industrialized on the English model, was the new 'liberal' kingdom of the Belgians. If the old-fashioned Calvinists had believed, to quote Robert Burns, that 'grace and gear' went together, the new optimistic utilitarians believed that wealth and freedom went together. Most, if not all Americans, for example, attributed the dramatic expansion of the American economy to republican liberties, and contrasted that expansion with what they asserted was the stagnation of Canada, sleeping under British rule.[1] Men of letters like Stendhal might sneer at the American passion for 'comfort', might shudder at the thought of living in the United States; but they did not doubt the comfort or doubt the existence of vast, fantastically increasing wealth. And even Stendhal wanted an imitation of British political institutions in France and Italy, although we may suspect he wanted much more radical changes than that as well. But if you wanted the new wealth being produced in Britain, the United States and, on a small scale, in Belgium, you had to have political institutions suitable for the new industrial society.

This political belief produced some odd judgements. More than one later commentator has made fun of Macaulay's praise of Leeds, at that time one of the most distressful specimens of the new industrial cities. Leeds, it is true, was Macaulay's parliamentary constituency; but there is no reason to believe that he was merely flattering his voters, as has been alleged. Romantic as he was, with many hankerings for the old order of things, he did believe that the future was and must be to the new industrial society. He welcomed all the new technical improvements even if he did not fully understand their impact and regarded progress as an inevitable straight line, culmina-

[1] Professor Daniel Boorstin has recently illustrated how much the rapid expansion of the United States was owing to defects as well as assets in the American way of life, e.g. the absence of skilled workmen, and how comparatively little was due to political institutions as such, although the absence of rigid political barriers was a great asset.

ting in the England of his day, although he admitted that the England of a century later would be very different and obviously very much better. It was this conviction that made him so confident that what India needed was remaking on the English model, that, confronted with that English model, the intelligent Indian had no real freedom of choice. He must needs choose the better when he saw it, and it was the business of the English to show it, above all, by teaching the English language. Macaulay's aim of producing 'brown Englishmen', to which I referred in my first lecture, was, in the context of Macaulay's general optimistic views, a perfectly rational and edifying assumption.

Even at the height of Victorian complacency, there were sceptical people. John Stuart Mill, who had read Coleridge as well as Bentham, and had many doubts about the results, for the great mass of people, of the growth of the industrial system. He had great doubts about the possibility of exporting to a country like India (for which he had very important official responsibilities) all English political and legal institutions. Walter Bagehot, the famous editor of the *Economist*, who also had close and important family relationships with India, said ironically that Adam Smith's theory of history was the progress of mankind from the state of barbarism to the state of being Scotchmen. This has always struck Englishmen and Americans as a good joke, although it is not much laughed at in my native land! And, of course, almost from the beginning there were 'socialist', 'communist', 'anarchist' critics of the new society, in England, in France, in Germany—even in the United States. The industrial revolution *was* a revolution; like all revolutions, very expensive; and many spectators and victims did not think the expense was justified by the results. Yet these were minority voices. They probably seem more important to us now than they did at the time of their utterance. The vogue for Coleridge, like the vogue for Marx, came long after. The general attitude of the

West to its own history and to the history of the backward parts of the world was one of complacent optimism and a simple faith that there were simple answers to fairly simple problems that hardly anyone shares today.

For example, that 'high and dry Whig', Henry Hallam the historian, although he was no radical and no democrat, *did* think there was a close connexion between his form of parliamentary liberalism, restricted as it was, and universal and natural progress. For him, the invention of representative government was an invention as important as, and as much of an invention—that is to say, a new discovery universally utilizable—as the steam engine. If the Romans had only had enough intelligence to think of representative government, or enough luck to stumble on the principle of the steam engine, the Roman Republic might not have declined into an imperial tyranny. For the basic problem, as Hallam saw it, was one of political mechanics. If in a political system in which all authority was in the hands of the Roman citizens, and could be exercised only in Rome itself, the large number of Roman citizens outside Rome were in fact disfranchised, the greater the extent of the rôle exercised by the Roman Republic, the greater the extension of the Roman franchise, the greater were the grievances of the Roman citizens who could not exercise their nominal rights. Parliamentary government would have solved all that!

Few of us are as simple-minded as Henry Hallam was; but it must be remembered that few of us are as intelligent as Henry Hallam was. His naïve error is educational because it shows how much we are all the children and the victims of our own age and of our own preconceived ideas.

But whatever might have happened to the Roman Empire, representative government had been discovered and had been exemplified in England and then in the United States. If we look at the *Federalist*, we can see that Madison's elaborate learning devoted to the problems of either adaptations of federal government or to the possibility of federal government on a large scale, provides mainly warnings rather then recipes. The secret of effective rule, in a free society over a large area, was a new secret to be discovered and exemplified in the new Constitution of the United States. The doubts and fears with which the new Constitution was greeted in America were shared also in Europe, although many of the fears in Europe were fears that the new republic would succeed, not that it would fail. Should the new republic succeed, a great deal of the old order in Europe would be doomed. But the new republic did not fail, and the liberalized monarchy of Britain did not fail after the first Reform Bill of 1832 (despite the alarms of Germanic philosophers like Hegel). The case seemed settled. The way to provide the political basis for economic expansion was to imitate the British constitution. Only radicals wished to imitate the American constitution, for its experience seemed irrelevant to the old, cabined and confined states of Europe. But that, in a sense, all the Western world must go the American way was the lesson of the most famous and most influential book on the United States ever published, Tocqueville's *Democracy in America.* He was more concerned with the spirit of equality than with the mechanics of government, but he thought that there was an indissoluble connexion between American growth and American political institutions.

But the rising middle classes of Europe, angered by the remaining archaic institutions which limited their economic development and social ascent, were also afraid of what they called 'the mob'; afraid of a repetition of the horrors of the first French Revolution; afraid that 'more democracy' would end in catastrophe. As Macaulay was to argue in his famous letter to Randall, America with its great natural resources could afford democracy; Europe could not.

But what Europe could afford was a bourgeois liberal government. The word 'bourgeois' was then not offensive, or offensive only in the mouths of painters, artists and musicians, of what were coming to be called 'bohemians', and are called at this moment 'beatniks' (the name may have changed by next year). The European middle classes, like the 'Third Estate' in 1789, were not everything, and they wanted to be everything. There were many signs of progress in a middle-class direction. There was the general adoption of trousers instead of knee breeches—hence the French Revolutionary term *sansculotte*. There was the adoption of middle-class morality. The courts of Louis-Philippe and Queen Victoria were very unlike the courts of eighteenth-century monarchs. If the English middle class adopted some of the habits of the life of the aristocracy, the aristocracy adopted some of the habits of the middle classes, above all their very high appreciation of money to be gained in business. There was no narrow prejudice in England against money earned in 'trade', *if* enough money was earned in trade, and *if* the founding father of the business was safely dead! This middle class took it as natural and right that its leadership would be accepted, reluctantly, by the declining aristocracy and increasingly feeble monarchs, and by the aspiring and intelligent working class. James Mill, the arid and almost inhuman father of John Stuart Mill, seems to have believed that the workers, like women and children, would accept the leadership of the middle-class millions, and what was good for the middle-class millions was good for the whole country and for everybody in it. The famous and, perhaps, misunderstood dictum of Mr. Charles Wilson about General Motors has, in fact, a long ancestry!

And this middle-class complacency had important political results, both inside the European state system and outside it. For one thing, it justified, or appeared to justify, what we now think of as imperialism. The most convinced, energetic, aggressive, and, in a way, successful missionaries of the West to India and China and then to Japan were, not the men moved by the desire to win India or China for Christ, but the men who wished to win India and China for business, and the commercial missionaries were not animated by much imperial zeal of the flag-waving type. The British businessman knew that he made more money in the United States than in any other country, and had no reason to believe that he could make more if the United States rejoined the Mother Country. In general, it was not true that 'trade followed the flag'; it was more that the flag followed trade as the traders wanted a government—any government—which would provide the minimum political conditions for the expansion of commerce.[1] Of course, in many parts of the world there were no government institutions which could provide a framework for the new intruders, for the 'young lighthearted masters of the waves', to borrow Matthew Arnold's description of the commercially and militarily aggressive Greeks. If there was to be a great expansion of the European market in Africa or Asia, or if there was to be a great increase in the import of raw materials from Asia or Africa, the European and American economic and legal systems had to be imposed by force. Sometimes it did not take very much force

[1] It is possible to argue plausibly that the only important colonial enterprise of the nineteenth century which was animated by missionary zeal in the religious sense was the establishment of French Indo-China, for this attracted as much of the missionary zeal of the French as did China, and produced a large number of martyrs; and French Catholics backed up an expansive policy in Indo-China less for its rather problematic profits than for the possibility of establishing a Catholic society on the flank of Asia. This Catholic obsession with Indo-China and with the church in Indo-China had extremely unfortunate results in 1945–7. It was very unfortunate, for instance, that Admiral Thierry d'Argenlieu, whom General de Gaulle sent out to recover the lost French colony, was a monk who had returned to the navy during the Second World War.

—for instance, in most of West Africa; sometimes it took a great deal of force, as in India and Indo-China. Sometimes the attempted imposition by force of effective legal and economic institutions failed, as French intervention in Mexico failed. But, roughly speaking, it was taken for granted that either native powers would adopt European institutions or that European powers—and from this point of view, the Americans were a European power—would impose the minimum conditions under which the new industrial society could work at a profit.

So the complacent Westerners invaded and acted as revolutionary forces all over the world. Sometimes they were consciously revolutionary forces, as the British East India Company was before the Great Mutiny of 1857. Its new legal system; its new educational system, making English the language of government; the organization of a new industrial system, e.g. the growing and the manufacture of cotton; above all, the coming of the railway, were revolutionary forces, and consciously revolutionary forces. Such Indian states as were allowed to survive were allowed to survive on the condition they did not interfere with the economic policy of the East India Company, and that policy was more and more the provision of conditions for private British enterprise rather than profit-making for the Company itself. After the Mutiny, the British government became alarmed at its revolutionary activity and began backing conservative forces in India—the native states, the Muslims, minority commercial groups like the Parsees, to some extent supporting the new and growing Indian business class, but on the whole leaving Indian society untouched by formal legislation. No British government in India would then have dared to make such inroads on native custom as the abolition of suttee and of thuggee. But, as Mr. Nehru pointed out, whether the post-Mutiny governments knew that or not, they were still revolutionary forces, bringing about the transformation of Indian society and a hostile reaction against British rule which ended in another revolution and the ending of British rule.

Where there were no possibilities of a takeover like the British takeover in India, or where the competition between the various imperialistically minded countries was too keen, the triumphant and aggressive West settled for a minimum of effective government in order to do a maximum of profitable trade. So we had the 'concessions' in China, and it might be remembered that the greatest and most successful of all concessions was the American concession in Shanghai. For America profited from this imperial penetration into China, as well as Britain and France, which took the onus—and the odium—of forcing China to trade with the West by force of arms.

Charles Gavan Duffy described Ireland after the Great Famine, as a 'corpse on the dissecting table'. This was an exaggeration of the tragic condition of Ireland, and it was a gross exaggeration of the placidity of the non-white world. For example, 'concessions' were an old feature of European dealings with the outside world. But they were genuine concessions by the sovereign power granting them; they were not alienations of sovereignty wrung from a defenceless state. The French, for example, had had their *comptoirs du Levant* for many hundreds of years. English rule in India began from 'factories' established on the edges of great native states, depending on those states for all their legal rights and all their possibilities of business and inhabited mainly by timid merchants who had no desire to offend, much less to anger, the native rulers. When the Manchu Empire, just passing its prime, began to deal with the intruding Westerners, notably the British and the Americans, it dealt with them in an extremely superior way, allowing them to deal with Chinese merchants in Canton but on terms in which all the inequality was on the Chinese side. The Japanese simply refused to do any trading at all with the outside world except with one concession made to the Dutch who, in order to trade, had ostentatiously to abandon the slightest suggestion of a desire to proselytize in favour of Christianity, a concession which the Dutch merchants were more ready to make than their more spiritually minded Spanish and Portuguese predecessors.

But after what unkind foreign commentators called 'the First Opium War', the rulers of China suddenly discovered that what they were now giving away, were not 'concessions' which could be limited and withdrawn at any moment, but parcels of Chinese sovereignty. Their illusions about their own military power, about the efficacy of their admirable archery were destroyed.[1]

Such were not the illusions of the more intelligent Japanese, who saw their Chinese mentors easily overwhelmed by a handful of Western barbarians. In a few years, the American squadron of Commodore Perry was to force on the Japanese, without an actual war, the same kind of concession and the same humiliations as the English had enforced on the Chinese. Japan, a much more intelligently governed state than declining China, had far more members of its ruling class who 'got the message' than had China. Even after the Second Chinese War, when the British and French together sacked Peking and burned the Summer Palace as a lesson to the 'Chinese barbarians', Chinese society proved inelastic, muscle-bound, and doomed to increasing victimization at the hands of the British, French, Americans and Russians. Soon, indeed, it was to know humiliation at the hands of its own cultural colony, Japan.

All over the world threatened by the aggressive Europeans and Americans, men of the educated classes at any rate, began to speculate on the sources of the strength of

[1] One of the illusions of the Chinese at this period was that by banning the export of rhubarb, they would cause a rise of constipation in England which would bring that country to its knees.

these aggressive barbarians and wonder, could their secret of power be acquired? Naturally, they did not set about learning from the West in any very amiable frame of mind. Resentments over a century old are still a source of passion and a source of policy today. Thus, the Turks began to resent the long-tolerated trading companies of the French and English. Thus, the Chinese feebly and the Japanese, with great energy and success, began to copy all that could be copied of the West. Thus the Indians, above all the high-class Hindus, began to copy their masters and learned from their masters with great success. What did they learn?

They learned a great many things, including, especially in Japan, a quick mastery of Western technology. But they also learned something more explosive than gunpowder: they learned Western ideas, or versions of Western ideas. And some of those ideas were gladly exported to the outside world by Europe and the United States with a very insufficient apprehension of the fact that the export might turn out to be a bad bargain for the exporters. Two ideas that were exported (far more successfully than Christianity) were what we can now roughly call 'democracy' and what we can far more confidently call 'nationalism'.

The more intelligent aggressors from the West, like the more intelligent members of the ruling classes in the continents so attacked, realized that one reason for the superiority of the West and one reason for the inferiority of Asia and Africa, was political. The influence of the French Revolution, we now know, spread farther and faster than we used to believe. It began, for example, to break up the nominal unity of the Muslim populations of the Ottoman Empire. The old Turkish bureaucratic state, with a bureaucracy consisting very largely of Greek and Armenian Christians, was not an adequate instrument for a modern Turkish state. Nor was a modern Turkish state the ideal which increasing numbers of 'Ottomans' (many of whom, of course, were Christians) wanted as a body politic to live under. The idea of the 'citizen' began to spread. And like a long, slow trail of gunpowder, it was to explode generations later.

In the same way, Hindu reformers, like the founders of the Brahma Samaj, began to wish to transform Indian society, preserving what was valuable and endurable in the old Indian way of life, but where there was a clash, choosing the new and manifestly successful Western way of life. Brahmin self-criticism more than Christian missionary effort ate into Indian society. As Macaulay had foreseen, introduction to Western ideas led to a change in political attitudes. The increasingly numerous and increasingly wealthy Indian classes educated in Western learning and science, began to have almost as laudatory a view of parliamentary government as had Henry Hallam. With the abolition of the East India Company in 1858, the British government and the British victor was confronted with the duty of ruling some two hundred million people[1] remote in space, different in history, different in religion, and—then possibly not as important as now—different in colour. This produced increasing perplexity in the British mind. More important, it produced increasing critical analysis and increasing political hopes in the Indian mind, or in that moving part of the Indian mind which was more and more turning to the West.

The same was true in Turkey, where various unconvincing and ineffective attempts to create a Western and almost a liberal state were made roughly from the time of President Andrew Jackson. There was a largely bogus

[1] The population of the Indian sub-continent when the first census was taken in 1868–76 was 236,548,350, made up of 188,249,455 in British India and 48,298,985 in the Indian native states not under direct British rule. At the census of 1961, the population of the Indian sub-continent was 532,955,695, made up of 439,235,082 in the Indian Union, 93,720,613 in Pakistan.

Western state established by the Albanian adventurer Mehemet Ali in Egypt. The works of John Locke, Montesquieu, and Rousseau began to be talked of, but not understood, all over Asia. In China, missionary effort, missionary schools, the sight of Shanghai and Tientsin, shook the millennial complacency of the Middle Kingdom. In Japan, at the risk of their lives, young Japanese began to escape to the West to experience, at first hand, that new society of which the Dutch traders had given them a glimpse. And, everywhere, the association between power and liberal institutions was made. If the word 'democracy' was not yet in general use, 'liberal' ideas were more and more fashionable and more and more potent. In the very arrogance of the claims they made for exemption from the ordinary rule of law that applied to the 'natives' in British India, British traders and adventurers taught the Indians the importance of the Rights of Englishmen, and in no very long time, the importance of the Rights of Man. National and personal humiliation, from Turkey to Japan, provoked, at first, a blind admiration for the West and a blind admiration for its political institutions. The West accepted as a due compliment the blind admiration, but showed little foresight as to the probable results of the imitation.

Today, it is extremely important that we should realize that even in those parts of the world in which our political institutions are consciously copied, and copied with some degree of success, they have been adapted and used as a weapon against the West, as a means of liberation from, and not merely as a means of assimilation to the predominant and, as we think, the obviously right culture. When we talk of 'the free world', we are talking of a world in which, in one sense, the majority of the human race never could want to join, and, in another sense, of a world which they resent or hate and wish to escape from or even to conquer. The days when highly sophisticated Hindus like the founders of the Indian Congress (whose chief teacher was a white member of the Indian Civil Service[1]) are over. The Indian Congress, today, is in one very important sense an importer and employer of Western political ideas, but its real strength comes from its success as a liberator from Western dominance.

Americans will say, and often do say, that they are not involved in this love-hate relationship. They have not been an imperial power; it is not against them the Turks and Indians and Chinese are revolting. This is an illusion. The rest of the world, that is, the non-white world, makes few fine distinctions. The Americans are part, and by now are by far the most important part, of the dominant white world. (Their only possible rivals for this title are the Russians!) The resentment of so many American Negroes against the 'Man' is a sample of the resentment of the majority of the human race as a class, even if, in some cases, it be modified by friendships with particular white men. One of the reasons for the painful disillusionment of the American people with China, is the discovery that the pupils of the missionaries took from their teaching only what was useful from the Chinese point of view, not from a Christian point of view, and least of all, from an American point of view.

In Latin America, all the resentments that the French, British, Dutch had accumulated in Asia are present and are concentrated on the United States. Much of the resentment of Latin America seems to me baseless. I don't think, for example, that the people of the Argentine Republic or even the people of Brazil have any serious and genuine grievances against the 'North Americans'. Much of the resentment is concealed self-criticism, an evasion of the question

[1] The founder of the Indian Congress, a retired British Indian Civil Servant named A. O. Hume, is as forgotten as Drexler, the founder of the German Workers' Party, formed in 1919 and renamed in 1921, when Drexler was replaced by Hitler, Nationalsozialistische Deutsche Arbeiterpartei, National Socialist German Workers' Party.

of why, with all their great resources, neither the Argentine Republic nor the United States of Brazil, has made nearly as much progress as an outside observer—or an inside observer—could have hoped for and could have expected. This kind of resentment is common enough all over the world. It is something that must be accepted, and if we regard it as unjust, it is not *totally* unjust or baseless.

It is of very great importance today to remember that the Western political recipe for success and Western claims to moral superiority are no longer universally accepted. It is not only that there is a rival recipe being pushed with great vigour on to the market, by two competing firms, Russia and China. That is a problem I must deal with later. It is, first of all, that the claims of the moral superiority of the West, terribly damaged in the First World War, have been ruined in the Second World War. It was the highly superior West that invented Buchenwald and Auschwitz. It was the highly superior West that bombed Hiroshima (and Dresden). Anyone from the West who goes preaching moral salvation to the heathen today asks for trouble—and gets it! It may have been his fundamentalist religion, with its profound sense of superiority over the heathen, that led to the death of John Birch, not Communist fear of his propaganda efforts as such.

As recently as 1914, it was possible to believe that the Western way of political life; of a government 'of equal justice under law'; of representative institutions; of a free press (an ambiguous term); of 'freedom slowly broadening down from precedent to precedent' or of being captured in one great rush,

> When Death was on thy drums, Democracy,
> And with one rush of slaves the world was free,

as Chesterton put it, was obviously right. All of these

illusions were illusions, even in 1914, but they were plausible illusions.

By 1918, they were even more illusory and much less plausible. It seems obvious, in retrospect, that the most important result of the First World War was not the creation of 'a world safe for democracy', but the Bolshehik Revolution. The simple continuity of the liberal tradition was broken. The American Revolution had proclaimed itself as *novus ordo seclorum*—a new order of the ages. The Bolshevik Revolution proclaimed itself as a new order of the ages and an ending of the old order far more complete than anything Jefferson or Franklin or Robespierre ever thought possible.

True, the illusion lasted for some time that it was the 'democratic powers' that had won the war. Too much attention was paid to the fall of the 'Czardom'. The disappearance of the Emperors—the German and the Austrian Kaisers, the Russian Czar—was less important than the appearance of Lenin. But the short lesson was that democracy paid off in war. So there was the short-lived experiment of the Weimar Republic in Germany; so there was the short-lived experiment of a liberal parliamentary government in Japan. So there was an awkward rapprochement between the Indian Nationalists and the British government. So there was a genuine extension of the areas, in Europe at any rate, where governments were based on the consent of the governed. Old nations came out of the tomb, as did Poland. What it may be not too offensive to describe as new nations, like Lithuania, came to birth. And there was a blind and naïve imitation of European and American political institutions all over the world.

It was believed, for example, that dictatorial governments in South America were on the way out; that Cuba was 'settling down'; that the Mexican revolution could be contained inside boundaries set down for it in Wall Street.

The United Fruit Company of Boston, like the United Africa Company of Liverpool and London, felt secure in its domains. These companies were not formally imperial powers, but they were really imperial powers, spiritual heirs of the East India Company and of the Hudson's Bay Company. If a great many things that did not happen had happened—if a great many things that did happen had not happened—the optimism that survived the defeat of Woodrow Wilson would have been justified.

After all, Turkey had become a republic. Egypt had become a constitutional monarchy. Nascent African nationalist movements were arising, but with aims well inside the boundaries laid down for them by African imperial powers, France and Britain. In the Congo, Belgium had abolished political problems by abolishing political rights for whites and blacks alike. In the Dutch East Indies, a slow, very slow, progress towards the extension of some political powers to the natives was under way. There were upheavals—for instance, in British India with horrors like the British massacre of Indians at Amritsar in the Punjab. But a world in which both Poland and Ireland had risen from the grave, was a world to encourage optimism.

The whole idea of an export of European and American political ideals and techniques was an illusion, a point I shall try to make later. But it is more important to emphasize the degree to which the adoption of Western ideas was the adoption of a tool, and not the adoption of the ideas and ideals of which the political mechanics were a derivative. Perhaps the truest comment on the illusions of the period between 1918 and 1929 is provided by the odd history of what are called the 'Cargo Cults'. After the last war, all over the Pacific islands, the American Navy, Army and Marines had strewn vast quantities of superfluous goods of all kinds. In these backward and poverty-stricken islands, this type of American wealth and wastefulness was regarded as a godsend. It was assumed that the Americans got these windfalls by praying to their gods. From the sky, from the sea, planes and ships had brought this astonishing variety of wealth to the true worshippers who were the Americans. During the war and after the war, the noble savages of the islands were also beneficiaries. But when the war ended, and the Americans left, the planes and ships came no longer. So, with simple and justifiable savage logic, the islanders prayed to the God of the cargoes and waited 'with golden expectations', as Wordsworth put it, of the French Revolution, for more cargoes. Their prayers were, alas, not answered!

It seems to me that the attitude of a great part of the outside world to the political and technical arts of the West, was a form of the 'cargo cult'. What was wanted was the results of the worship by the white men, of their strange gods. What was *not* wanted, was the philosophical and theoretical bases of Western achievements. Democracy, from this point of view, was a kind of Aladdin's lamp. New lamps for old would bring the wealth and power of the West. It did not turn out to be like that, and the automatic acceptance of the political superiority of the West, of the 'free world', was a thing of the past. The vast majority of the human race were not concerned with the problems of Henry Hallam or of John Stuart Mill, of Montesquieu or of Jefferson. They sought wealth, health, the possibility of present happiness. And they also sought, as well, revenge for the inflictions on their pride which the West had practised since Columbus first entered the Caribbean and Vasco da Gama first entered Indian waters.

So when we talk to the vast majority of the human race today of the 'free world', we are not talking to a captive audience, but to an audience conditioned by historical experience to regard everything we say with suspicion, if not with bitter and possibly incurable hostility. We used to have the resources and the power; we no longer have that undividedly and we do not have now what we have never had, a genuine acceptance of our world philosophy and of the set of political institutions which we ambiguously call democracy.

III

IT is one of the handicaps of the Western powers today, of the ex-imperial powers like France and Britain, and still more one of the handicaps of the United States, that since 1917 the automatic acceptance of the superiority of Western political models has ceased. It is still very common, in the United States for instance, to see this as an abnormal and transitory situation. If the world is no longer to be won for Christ in this generation, it can be won, or recovered, for democracy. There is a black and white view of the world (not racial) in which the natural and self-evident fruits of Western political institutions are threatened by what must be, in the nature of things, a dishonest, disastrous, and ignoble rivalry. This is to put things much too simply.

To reiterate a platitude, the Western world never recovered its automatic moral superiority after the First World War. The rising educated classes of the non-white world would have had to be extremely unobservant not to question the claims made so confidently by their masters before 1914. Most of these claims had been accepted before 1914; the Western model was the model aimed at by revolutionary leaders, or even reformist leaders, in Japan, in China, in Latin America, in Turkey, and, although at this time fairly peaceably, in Africa. For example, at the time of the Indian Mutiny in 1857, the small but growing class of Indians who had received a Western education was strongly on the side of the British. For they saw the Mutiny not as a great patriotic revolt, but as an attempt to put the clock back, to restore the archaic and rightly condemned rule of the Princes of the Moghul

Empire, a result detestable alike to many Muslims and most high-caste Hindus. The victory of the British was welcomed in the business and professional classes in Calcutta, Bombay and Madras. There was no regret at the final destruction of what was left of the Moghul Empire and the 'Kingdom of Delhi'. The future was to the great trading cities founded by the British.

In the same way, the 'Concessions' in China, Tientsin and Shanghai and the other treaty ports, were sources of political propaganda even when these Concessions were ruled in a spirit very offensive to the Chinese themselves. Each disaster that befell the old Chinese order—the wars waged by Britain and France against the imperial power; the Taiping rebellion; the constant threat to the northern boundaries of the Empire from the Russians, and to the southern boundaries in what was then called Indo-China by the French—induced more and more intelligent Chinese to question their own political order, and to plan to imitate the successful political order of the West. Such were the ideas of Sun Yat-sen at the end of the nineteenth century; such were the motives of the reformers humiliated by the easy defeat of Imperial China at the hands of Japan.

In the same way, the Japanese themselves felt it necessary to imitate a great deal of the political methods of the West. True, they did not imitate the political methods of the democratic West. They were more impressed by Prussia than by Britain or France or the United States. A Prussian constitution made it easier to carry on the ingenious system of government which, by exulting the divine emperor, allowed Japan to carry out its modernization programme with only one serious internal rebellion to contend with. The defeat of the Satsuma Samurai by the new imperial peasant soldiery was, in a sense, a democratic triumph, but it was a democratic triumph in a highly oligarchical and spiritually very undemocratic society.

But the victory over Russia, which had such great repercussions all over Asia, was a victory of a society more advanced in the Western direction than any other Asiatic power over a very backward Western country still clinging to an archaic form of absolutism. The Mikado was a modern ruler compared with the Czar. And when, to the surprise of many Japanese, especially of the army, the Germans finally lost the First World War, there was a movement towards imitating the political institutions of the victors and abandoning the institutions of the vanquished. So there was a formal adoption of something like liberal democracy in Japan. (There was, for example, for the first time, a non-noble prime minister.) The effective ruling power in Japan seemed to have passed to the great business classes and out of the hands of the feudal clans who had made the Meiji restoration. And it is possible that if this liberalized but not democratic Japan had secured more visible external gains; if it had felt itself free to expand economically without running up against the barriers raised, on the one hand, by the old imperial powers on the mainland of Asia, and by the United States in the Pacific, there *might* have been a slow evolution of the imperial system towards something like the constitutional monarchies of Europe. And again, as has so often to be said, if there had not been the great economic crash of 1929 spreading all over the world and disastrously proving the unity of the new world economic system, Japan might have avoided its disastrous descent into a reckless imperialism, the suppression of the sagacious and prudent business and diplomatic leaders and the heirs of the old Genro, the 'elder statesmen', by the army and navy officers, the 'double patriots'. (The navy, trained on British models, was far less fanatical and credulous than was the army, trained on German models; and if the Japanese navy was no longer afraid of the British navy, it had a very great respect for the American navy.) But the great crash did come; it is hard to see how the Japanese folly could have been avoided. Now, in addition to the moral discredit which the West suffered from the spectacle of the First World War, was the discredit of its economic system. And as the value of the political institutions of the West had been connected in the minds of the rising middle classes everywhere in the world with its economic supremacy, the apparent collapse of the economic system discredited the political institutions.

But this speculation is, perhaps, fruitless. For the overthrow of the Czarist Empire, the collapse of the privileged position in East Asia of one of the greatest white powers, the degree to which things that were thought impossible of attainment in 1914, seemed well within reach in 1920, opened a revolutionary era in which we are still living.

First of all, a point that is very often forgotten today, the success of the Bolsheviks in turning the parliamentary and Western first Russian Revolution into a brand-new type of revolutionary organization based on 'the dictatorship of the proletariat'—in fact, on the dictatorship of the small oligarchical Communist Party—was in the West for a time a scandal—as much a scandal to many socialists as to conservatives and liberals. But it was also a temptation.

After many years of preaching revolution and not only failing to achieve it, but obviously getting further away from the revolutionary temper and revolutionary aims each year, the credit of the left wing and now fundamentally non-revolutionary parties in Europe was very badly shaken. People driven to moral and emotional despair by the collapse of international pacifist hopes in 1914; by the disillusionment, inevitable in any event with the results of the 'war to make the world safe for democracy' or the 'war that will end war' were ready, for longer or shorter periods, for a blind admiration of the group which *had* made a revolution; which *had* got out of the war; which promised to remake a world that obviously had a great deal wrong with it. The scandal caused by the Bolshevik dissolution of the Russian Constituent Assembly in 1918 was soon forgotten in the general wave of disillusionment which followed on the collapse of Wilson's campaign, the realization that the bills for the war had now to be paid, that the aim of creating, in England, a country fit for heroes to live in, had turned out to be, as was bitterly said, to make a country in which only heroes could live.

This created a demand for some solution to problems that seemed desperately urgent and desperately difficult in 1920. Then the universal collapse of the hopes fostered by government propaganda on both sides in the Great War, made people willing to believe in an alternative panacea. No governments had ever demanded as much of the governed as the governments of Europe did between 1914 and 1918. No governments had been so successful in dissipating the assets of their subjects. Few governments had as little to show for all this as the governments of the victors and the vanquished alike in 1919. There is nothing surprising or discreditable or historically accidental in the way in which so many of the 'intellectuals', the heirs of the 'intelligentsia' which had had such an apparent triumph in Russia 'fell' for the Bolshevik legend. Now was the day of salvation, so long preached, so long hoped for, so recently despaired of. To the young and youngish men who had protested against the war of 1914 as futile butchery, the only gain of the bloody mess was the liberation of Russia. Naturally, this belief was strongest among Jews who had had so many reasons to loathe and fear the Czardom. But it won over incurable romantics like Romain Rolland, incurable posturers like Anatole France, incurable sceptics like Lincoln Steffens who could ignore the kind of future whose working he saw because he was so completely disillusioned with the Western, especially the American, present. Many naïve workers and workers' leaders welcomed the red dawn. French politicians, thinking that the new Third International was as rhetorical and empty an organization as the Second, hastened to proclaim 'no enemies on the Left', only to discover that the new Left intended to be a master not an ally. Men like Zinoviev laid down the law; men like Marquet for a time accepted it.

Thus in Britain in 1924, it was orthodox doctrine on the Left of the Labour Party that the 'Zinoviev letter' *must* be a forgery (there was no reason why it need have been), only for them to discover later that Zinoviev was as black a traitor as Ramsay MacDonald.

The chances of a successful revolution were grossly exaggerated, especially by ex-pacifists in the 'Anglo-Saxon' countries. The English working class were told and believed that they had saved the Soviet government by a minor strike and waited with some complacency for the Red Army to overrun that artificial creation of the wicked French and the naïve Wilson, Poland (so inferior to Czechoslovakia). And up to the defeat of the Red Army outside Warsaw in 1920 these hopes were not obviously foolish. After that defeat, it was evident to the less doctrinaire Communist leaders in Russia, that the chances of a general proletarian revolution in Europe were not at the moment good. Attempts were made, it is true, to exploit deteriorating situations—for example, in Germany in 1923. But the capitalist system and even liberal democracy had a lot more life in them than seemed probable at the end of 1919. More than that, where the Western proletarian parties *had* attempted revolution, they were defeated. The decadent bourgeoisie turned out to be a more formidable force than the emergent proletariat.

What we now call Fascism became a powerful rival, and in some countries a triumphant rival, of Communism, as well as an effective enemy of all liberal traditions and institutions. So the prestige of the systems of government which many people had expected in the first quarter of the twentieth century to see spread all over the world, was vitally affected, by revolution and by counter-revolution.

We can see that Lenin was historically a far more important and far greater man than Mussolini, but to a great part of the world Lenin and Mussolini were teaching the same lesson, that force—what would a few years before have been called tyranny—*did* answer a great many questions, that political authority was, to use an Americanism, 'up for grabs' in many countries; that the cake of custom was very thin. If the habit of obedience was lost or the habit of naïve faith in the rights of man and the rest of the liberal tradition was weakened, it was not at all certain which of the enemies of these traditional doctrines would triumph.

But it seems clear today that the significance of the Russian Revolution and of Fascism was not in Western Europe and not in the United States where neither was even a starter, but in the rest of the world, in what was to be called the under-privileged world. The leaders of reformist liberal or even revolutionary parties in countries like Turkey, Indo-China, Japan were, in the main, middle-class intellectuals envying the rôle of middle-class intellectuals in England, France, or the United States. The changes they looked forward to were changes directed to extending the rôle of the middle class, as exemplified, for example, in the formal power of Mr. Hara in Japan. The movement towards Western institutions which had produced the creation of the Duma in Russia, of the Majlis in Persia, of the Turkish parliament, and led to agitation in India for the creation of comparable institutions, was now being replaced by far more formidable forces. All of these liberal movements had been, in one sense, nationalist in origin. It was defeat in war that caused the Czardom to make its first concessions towards liberal institutions in 1905. It was a sense of impotence and of humiliation that forced concessions from the decadent imperial rulers of Turkey and of Persia. It was not only because the decadent Ch'ing dynasty in China had not been able to protect Chinese autonomy from the aggressions of the West, but had not been able to exploit effectively the explosion of anger over the humiliations that China underwent in the Boxer rebellion, that the Chinese intellectuals, more and more influenced by the example of Japan, decided that the 'mandate of heaven' had been withdrawn from the Manchu dynasty.

Far more revolutionary than a mere change of dynasty—a common enough phenomenon in Chinese history over thousands of years—was the decision of this increasingly important and disillusioned class that the old Confucian governmental structure had failed; that the question of what family exercised imperial power was irrelevant to the modern world. The mandarinate and the classical examination system, the complacency with which 'the Middle Kingdom' regarded the rest of the world as barbarian, all of this was now subject to a violent revolutionary criticism.

This desire for reform on what one might call the Japanese conservative model was replaced by the genuinely revolutionary enthusiasm let loose by the Russian Revolution and by the collapse of the Czardom. It was not only that the Bolsheviks abandoned the preferential status that imperial Russia had secured in China, above all in Manchuria, but that possibilities were now open of a *real* revolution appealing to the great masses of the peasantry, a kind of Taiping rebellion with a modern doctrine. True, misled by the Russian analogy in which power had been seized by small groups of townspeople, the first Communist wave in China was defeated and Russian leadership was discredited. But the dyke had burst and Chinese Communist leaders refused to follow the Russian recipe. They tapped the great pool of peasant misery and peasant hopes. What that meant, the future was to show.

The same change in the character of the reformist movement or of the imitation of the West can be seen in India. Gandhi was a new type of Indian revolutionary. Of course, trained in the law in London, practising the law in South Africa, a master of English, Gandhi was not a peasant leader (he was, in fact, the son of the prime minister of a small native state); but he exemplified in his person the new nationalist revolution in India which was not a matter of simply westernizing India, but in part a matter of reversing the trend which under British rule had already gone a long way. Many of his followers, especially the most prominent of them, Pandit Nehru, were Westerners by education and conviction who yet thought that they could not shake British rule in India or replace it or secure 'freedom' without the kind of appeal which only the Mahatma had. So that the force which increasingly weakened British authority in India was no longer one simply attempting to secure for India the kind of institutions which it might be held had been promised as far back as 1858 and were implicit in Macaulay's language and education policy. For Gandhi's strength was partly the strength of archaism. By putting off Western clothes at the risk of being described as 'a naked fakir', by preaching home crafts, by exalting the severities of Indian peasant life, by preaching pacific resistance to British authority, Gandhi was both a revolutionary and a reactionary force. And the force he created was the result of national and religious feeling as well as of a desire for modernization or a desire for social justice such as appealed to men like Pandit Nehru who were still deeply in the Western tradition. The Indian business class, the Indian official class, Indian academics were, many of them, probably most of them, sceptical of the 'archaism' of Gandhi's propaganda and programmes; but he alone could move the hundreds of millions of the Indian poor. And he certainly did not move them with a view to establishing simply a liberal westernized Anglicized India which was formally free, but culturally enslaved. What Gandhi would have made of free India had he survived a few years after the British withdrawal in

1947, no one knows; but he almost certainly would have been disillusioned by it as more homage is paid to his memory than to his precepts. But Gandhi as a revolutionary figure was unlike the great revolutionary figures before 1914. He was not in the least, despite his English education, planning to bring India into the twentieth century. He had a very sceptical view of the merits of the twentieth century!

It was evident by round 1930 that the really powerful forces at work in the world were what may be called Communist or Socialist or Nationalist; and the most powerful forces were those which combined a socialist and a nationalist appeal. One or other or both might be bogus; when the forces clashed, it was nationalism which as a rule won. If, in the breakdown of authority and normal expectations which accompanied the great depression and then the Second War, nationalism did not always win, it was because what was now in effect a new nationalist state, Soviet Russia, was able to suppress rival nationalisms inside its borders and on the edges of its formal frontiers. And nationalism was a doctrine no longer associated with liberalism; no longer a matter of establishing governments with the consent of the governed. It was a political religion, uncritical, emotional and highly dangerous.

Before 1914, nationalism had gone hand in hand with what the liberals called 'progress'. Although Bismarck's triumph of unifying Germany by very illiberal means shocked the faith of the innocent believers in progress, it could be held that imperial Germany was slowly and erratically moving towards a kind of parliamentary democracy. Nationalism in the First War and after proved more potent than any appeal to liberal ideas as such. Part of the success of the Bolsheviks in Russia was due to their exploitation of nationalist feeling against the invading Allies, against the Poles, against the possibly fictitious legend of economic imperialism attempting to destroy the autonomy of the Russian people. The rise of Fascism in Italy was made possible by the humiliations that as a formally victorious power, Italy suffered after the First War; and the rise of the Nazis in Germany was almost entirely based on nationalist emotional appeals of which anti-Semitism, a definition of Germanism by exclusion, was one of the most powerful.

All over the world, it was nationalism that shook the existing order. It broke up the unity of Islam when there was a clash between Turkish and Arab aims. It broke up the unity of India when there was a clash between Muslim and Hindu aims. For it was a national problem, rather than a strictly religious problem, that led to the destruction of the greatest British achievement, the unity of India. So the triumph of nationalism often produced more nations than had been foreseen when the movements began, and produced nations that might not have come into existence but for the provocation of older nationalisms.

In Latin America, the negative source of unity or hostility, 'Yanquí imperialism', was one of the few unifying forces. In Mexico, the Latin American country which had the nearest approach to a successful revolution, there was the deliberate exploitation not only of hostility to the Yanquís, but to the relics of Spanish racial supremacy; there was an appeal to the Indian past (unconsciously parodied by D. H. Lawrence in *The Plumed Serpent*). And in none of these countries was there any question of sacrificing national aims, wise or foolish, well-founded or fictitious, to any mere principle of 'liberty' or the 'rights of man' in the old traditional sense. So at a time when one might have expected, in a rapidly changing world, the achievement of the hopes of the nineteenth century, of the export of the best political institutions, that is, those of Western Europe and North America, the market suddenly disappeared.

It is very hard for people born in the early years of this century (which includes most of the rulers of the Western

world) to accept this fact. It was easy in the last century to quote Tennyson complacently, 'better fifty years of Europe than a cycle of Cathay'. It was assumed that Cathay would either not change, or would be changed corrosively by the foreign powers who had descended on China; and the changes would necessarily be, unless they had been totally disastrous for China, changes in the direction of the Western liberal tradition.

For the reasons already given, it has not turned out like that. But we tend still to regard as a temporary aberration what is almost certainly a permanent change in world history. It is not likely that anyone now alive will see the success of the policy of westernizing 'backward regions' any more than they will see the winning of the world for Christ. Indeed, Western policy, especially American policy, has become the policy defined by George Kennan in a famous article as 'containment'. Whatever may be said, no one outside the United States, and fewer and fewer people inside it, believe in the fiction of the overthrow of 'Red China' by the rulers, possibly the temporary rulers, of Formosa, or the restoration of the highly unsatisfactory *status quo*, if it can be called that, which existed at the end of the American victory over Japan when it was possible to believe that the Kuomintang would in fact be the heir of the Japanese Empire in China.

The heir was not the Kuomintang; it was not even Moscow. It was an indigenous Chinese movement, strongly influenced by Marxism it is true, but answering deep Chinese needs. Any foreign policy today which ignores this fact and thinks that one of the great decisive victories of history, the emergence of a unified, powerful, and technological state in China can be reversed, is imagining a vain thing. We should learn this: as China becomes a dangerous atomic power, we may have good reasons to learn it; but we cannot change it. The domination of China by a party far more unified and far more competent for its job than the Kuomintang ever was may well be the single most important result of the Second World War. As Americans should always remember, there are three Chinese for every American. And, indeed, the real reply to the common American query, 'Why did we lose China?' is 'Why has China not yet won the United States?'

I do not believe that the United States is in danger of any successful Chinese takeover bid, but even to reflect on why the United States is not in danger is to make obvious the absurdity of the old complaint that by treason, incompetence, liberal illusions, the United States 'lost China'. It was not theirs to lose. It is unlikely that even the temporary Japanese domination of a great part of the country would have endured for very long. The comparative ease with which the British, the French, the Japanese defeated the Chinese armies and navies, the comparative ease with which other powers like the United States imposed themselves on China, filched a great part of Chinese property by what the Chinese called 'unequal treaties' was simply an episode common enough in Chinese history when one political structure was decaying rapidly and the succeeding dynasty had not yet established itself. By Chinese standards, the time taken from the revolution of 1912 to the effective establishment of Communist rule in 1949 was not very long. It was, in fact, less than 'fifty years of Europe'!

Much less important, but of almost equal interest, has been the narrowing of the impulse for white political institutions of the traditional liberal type in other parts of Asia and in Africa. Indeed, many apologists for the new African states and many defenders of such new and conspicuously ill-governed Asiatic states as Indonesia, excuse disastrous and expensive errors, excuse an economic decline which is very alarming, in terms that are possibly insulting to the peoples of Africa and Asia. It was thought unkind of John Stuart Mill, 'the saint of rationalism', as

Gladstone called him, to assert that the best government India could hope for was the kind of government provided by a Charlemagne or an Akbar. But the same kind of criticism of the new emerging states is quite good form today, especially among professional liberals. It is they who assert that we must welcome as a necessary stage in progress (if it is to be no more than that) the establishment of one-party, authoritarian states and the cultivation of a 'cult of personality' which the Russians have officially renounced since the death of Stalin. It is unkind to recall liberal criticisms of the adulation and adoration of Mussolini and Hitler. But that adoration and adulation have been offered and gratefully accepted and indeed fostered by Dr. Nkrumah and Dr. Sukarno, each of whom received an advanced Western education and had at any rate been exposed to, if not much affected by, Western liberal ideas of the traditional kind. The instability of many of the new states and the confident claim that they are held together only by encouraging this political idolatry of one man is a great deception of Western hopes.[1]

It is also, as Professor Arthur Lewis has suggested, a betrayal of many African hopes. That very distinguished Negro economist from Jamaica has expressed the view that the readiness with which enlightened Western opinion accepts régimes like that of Dr. Nkrumah is a new form of racial arrogance. The political religion imposed on Ghana is an insult to many of the more educated Ghanaians; and it has been unkindly suggested that it represents a resentment among the large semi-literate class of the literate class who are as much hated and despised as the old instruments of imperial rule were. Some Africans, like Dr. Busia, have made the same complaint, and in few of the African states are what used to be called the 'rights of man' any

[1] At the time these lectures were given, I did not foresee the collapse of the authority of Dr. Sukarno after the failed Communist takeover bid.

better secured than they were under French, British or even Belgian 'tyranny'.

It was ironical and painful to see the authority of the legal and 'democratic' governments of British East Africa restored by British troops after the outbreak of mutiny in the new armies of these states. The record of the Congo army is not edifying. Neither is the record of the military forces in some of the French ex-colonies. It is therefore doubtful whether political progress in Africa can be achieved by the use of the old-fashioned liberal recipes. But it is also doubtful if it can be achieved by the new dictatorial, one-party governments which, while much less wicked, have a disturbing resemblance to those of Nazi Germany and Fascist Italy.

One can understand the indignation of Professor Lewis and Dr. Busia, for they are the kind of Negro intellectuals the new leaders suspect and of whom they are possibly jealous. But the chances of democratic government of the Western type, especially of the British and French parliamentary type, are not at the moment good. And this is a cause of general disillusionment with the emerging nations in the rich countries whose aid is absolutely essential for preventing the emerging nations from going backwards economically, not forward. It is also a source of disillusionment in Africa and Asia where the results of independence have not been at once transformed into tangible economic and cultural gains. The attitude that the former imperial powers, and above all the United States, which only in its own eyes is not an imperial power, should take is one of the most serious problems of Western or, to be candid, white foreign policy.

In dealing with these problems, the United States, or at any rate the American people, suffered a serious handicap because of the completeness of their faith in their own political institutions. More than one commentator on America has pointed out that it is a nation founded on a creed, expressed in the Declaration of Independence. It is a nation whose constitution is not merely a system of political arrangements, but a sacred document; a form of Holy Writ.[1]

It is natural for the American people and tempting for the American government, to judge nations which are competing for goodwill or aid, or threatening American interests, by rather naïve verbal tests. For example, it was long true that a great many Americans thought 'the United States of Mexico' (or 'the United States of Brazil') was free in a sense that 'the Dominion of Canada' was not. For Canada had both colonial and monarchical institutions; it therefore could not be free like a republic which was legally independent of every other state in the world. Sometimes the difference between Canada and Mexico was seen in rather comic terms. Thus, as late as 1939, it was discovered by an ingenious poll-taker that about half the American people believed that Canada paid tribute to Great Britain, and, what was more astonishing, that a large proportion of the population of Detroit believed this although you can walk into Canada from Detroit in about five minutes.

American popular judgement, and consequently American policy, have been affected, and affected disastrously, by this 'realism' in the medieval sense. The 'realists' of the Middle Ages were, in fact, the very opposite of what we should call realists. They believed that words, phrases, dogmatic statements represented real things even when they represented nothing but words. And the American people and the American government, especially such leaders of the American government as John Foster Dulles, believed, and many still believe, in the 'reality' of very ambiguous or, indeed, nearly meaningless phrases like 'the American way of life'; 'the free enterprise system'; 'demo-

[1] As far as I know, the United States is the only government which has a double dating system for important documents, 'the year of the Lord' and the 'year of the independence of the United States'.

cratic institutions'. This does not mean that these phrases have no meaning at all; but the kind of meaning they have ought in every instance to be carefully scrutinized. And it should always be remembered that there is no political equivalent to the Detroit assembly line; no political equivalent to perhaps the greatest of American technical innovations, the invention of absolutely interchangeable parts.

No governmental machine in any country, however successful in that country, consists of a series of parts to be used repeatedly on a political assembly line. This is not to say that there are no political spare parts that can be used, more or less efficiently, in a political machine other than that for which they were originally designed. Thus, it is not accidental that the various British colonies or dependencies which have achieved independence have almost all attempted to imitate the British parliamentary system, and many have attempted it with success. It is not unimportant, for example, that when the Irish Free State was established, a gallant attempt was made to give it institutions unlike those of the British parliamentary system; very quickly the Irish parliament and the Irish executive government became very like the House of Commons and the British cabinet.

Yet, in Canada, in Australia, in New Zealand, the variations on the British parliamentary model are important. The House of Commons in Ottawa is like, but very far from identical with the House of Commons at Westminster or the House of Representatives at Canberra. The *Lok Sabha* in Delhi is, one is told, quite like the House of Commons at Westminster.[1] But if it has been impossible to transfer British political institutions with their long, continuous and, on the whole, successful history to new societies which are connected in almost every way with the

[1] Since giving this lecture, I have seen the *Lok Sabha* in session in Delhi, and it is certainly more like the House of Commons than like the American House of Representatives.

society which produced the British system, how much more difficult it is to export these institutions to societies which have been under British rule, but have had only the most primitive and mechanical of British institutions to live under. It is because India was the richest, the most advanced, the most studied of the British colonies, that the British government, or some leaders of it, tried to train the increasingly numerous Indian educated class in its own political traditions that India alone of all the great modern countries of Asia, has preserved a great deal of British institutions like 'the rule of law', like 'a free press', like—at the top at any rate—a very competent and incorruptible civil service.[1]

But if it has been difficult to do more than export parts of the British political system to populations associated as subjects, if not as citizens, with the British imperial government, how much more difficult has been the rôle of the United States in exporting *its* political institutions!

Of course, the United States has had very great influence, for example in Latin America, in China, and, to a less degree, in Japan, for a very long time. But 'influence is not government'. The United States prides itself on not having an imperial past, on not expanding its political power by arms when it could easily have done so. From the Mexican point of view, the United States might seem to have been in the past an extremely aggressive power. From the American point of view, it may seem to have been a very moderate power since after the complete defeat of Mexico and the practical destruction of the primitive Mexican state in 1846–8, the United States showed remarkable moderation. It is due to that moderation that Mexico and the United States have had their difficulties over the control

[1] I once heard Mr. De Valera express the view that the Indian Civil Service (of British times) was the best civil service in the world. This can be neither proved nor disproved, but was an interesting and not implausible judgement.

of the mouth of the Colorado River, because it is certain that a European power as completely in command as the United States was in 1848 would have solved the question by annexing Lower California and the mouth of the Colorado.

And if it can be said that the United States gained as much by the imposition of the unequal treaties on China as did France and Britain, it was in fact Britain and France which fought China. If it was the United States that forced the opening of Japan, it was as much France and Britain as the United States that continued the pressure, that pressure sometimes taking the form of warfare. And there is no doubt that the United States provided a great deal of the vocabulary of resistance to imperial power; there is no doubt that a great many politicians quite sincerely saw and see an almost identical pattern of behaviour exemplified by the American colonists in the eighteenth century and many nations 'rightly struggling to be free'[1] in the twentieth.

But when Dr. Sukarno uses the words of Jefferson or of Lincoln, he is using them in a new sense. He is concerned only with the establishment of the independence of Indonesia or, to be more exact, the creation of Indonesia out of the débris of the Dutch East Indies, but no more than Dr. Nkrumah is he concerned with the principles and practices enshrined in the American Bill of Rights, or in the French Revolutionary Declaration of the Rights of Man and the Citizen.

For one basic truth which must be accepted, however reluctantly, is that for a great part of the world today it is true that 'good government is no substitute for self-government'. If the disillusioned former imperial powers —disillusioned with their own record and then disillusioned with the record of the liberated countries—begin to doubt themselves, the liberated peoples do not. For them it is as true as the basic truth stated by Byron:

[1] This famous phrase comes from William Ewart Gladstone, not Thomas Jefferson.

A tyrant—but our masters then
Were still at least our countrymen.[1]

But it must be remembered that if imperialism was wicked, a defiance 'of the laws of Nature and of Nature's God', it was not totally nefarious in its results. It could be argued indeed that the countries which were not directly ruled by the imperial powers suffered worse than those which were directly ruled. Persia, for example, was less well governed by its native and decaying government than it would have been had it been conquered by either England or Russia, and it was saved from a fate much better than death, as was Thailand, by the rivalry of the imperial powers. It may be argued, too, that open American imperialism in Latin America would have been better than the support given by American Big Business to the 'Porfiriato' of Díaz in Mexico or to the various dictators who were appointed and, according to that veracious authority, O. Henry, deposed by the United Fruit Company of Boston.

Imperialism imposes responsibilities, and these responsibilities were better accepted when the imperial power was democratic at home. The slow reforms in the Dutch Indies were imposed by the democratic politicians of the Netherlands; the worst scandals of King Leopold II's rule in the 'Congo Free State' were abolished when the democratic government of Belgium took direct responsibility for what had been the King's private estate and ruled it in a very undemocratic way, but very much better than it had been ruled by the King, and possibly very much better than it would have been ruled, at that time, by any conceivable African authority.

[1] It is a sign of sophistication when a very distinguished Irish author like Sean O'Faolaín, discussing the question of the English conquest of Ireland in the sixteenth century, calmly suggests that for many of the Irish peasantry, if not for the Irish nobility, English rule may have been an improvement!

To sum up, the illusions to be avoided are that the old automatic technical, economic, religious, and political superiority of the West is any longer accepted as the nature of things. It is also to be noted that from the point of view of the greater part of the world, the United States is an imperial power, if not of the same kind, of the same character as were the old imperial powers, Britain, France, the Netherlands, Belgium, Russia. It has to be accepted that not all the results of imperialism were bad, but—what is less disputable—that many of its results are still with us and cannot be ignored or abolished by the mere shouting of slogans, even if those slogans use the language of the American or the French Revolutions.

If many things had happened which did not happen and many things had not happened which did happen, it is possible that the desperate dilemmas facing the United States as well as Europe would not be facing them. If there had been no First World War, there might have been a slow adjustment of imperial power; if there had been no Russian Revolution, there might have been a slow adjustment of society within Russia, a great Asiatic as well as a great European power. If there had been no Russian Revolution—or at any rate if there had been no Bolshevik Revolution in Russia—the inevitable Chinese revolution, while it would never have taken the simple liberal route laid down for it by Sun Yat-sen in his early years, might have been more peaceful, and have been far less expensive in life, liberty and happiness. If there had been no Second World War, the present-day collapse of the imperial structure in Asia and Africa might not have taken place, and that might not have been a totally bad thing. But, as we say in my native Scotland,

> If ifs and ans
> Were pots and pans,
> There'd be nae ca' for tinkers!

IV

ONE of the great difficulties of a commentator of my age, and one of the great difficulties of an audience, for the most part so much younger, is the tricks of memory that age plays. I can remember very easily when in the United States the Republican Party was the automatic majority party, and even now I still find it a little difficult to realize that this has long ceased to be the truth. I can still remember many members of the political personnel in Great Britain, France, the United States who ruled, or at any rate presided over, the destinies of nations between the two wars. I am even old enough to remember some of the leaders towards the end of the First War. These are purely historical figures, as remote as Lincoln and much less living memories, to most Americans today. Alas, very soon one's mind becomes rigid and the patterns of one's youth and early manhood become fixed. In this way we all have one-track minds; we are on one historical track. The engine is still running, but we are mentally at the first or second station on the line.

This is one of the causes of the differences between the rulers and the ruled in all democratic states. One of the reasons for the world attraction towards John Kennedy was simply that he had been born towards the end of the First World War; that he had served as a very junior officer in the Second World War; and that although he was not, in the ordinary sense of the term, a young man when he entered the White House, he was the youngest man ever to be elected President, and compared with the other world leaders—with the British Prime Minister Macmillan, with President de Gaulle, with Khrushchev, with Mao Tse-tung, with almost everybody—he was boyish. And I am convinced that many of our psychological problems, the problems of the mutual education of seniors and juniors arise naturally from this gap in experience. This has doubtless always been so, but the speed of change is so great today and the duration of life so much longer that the differences of generations matter more than they have done in any historical epoch known to me. In a crisis of the troubled history of the Third Republic in France, a leading politician rebuked an ambitious general by saying, 'At your age, General Boulanger, Bonaparte was dead'; and it is hard to remember that at Waterloo, Wellington and Napoleon were the same age as John Kennedy when he was assassinated.

Equal in importance to this gap between the generations of rulers and ruled is the speed with which great historical events take place and pass into history. It is hard to remember that Franklin D. Roosevelt was President of the United States for a longer period than Napoleon was Emperor of the French or Hitler Führer of the German Reich. It is hard to remember that Alexander the Great died just a little after the age which would have admitted him to the United States Senate as a newcomer. When Caesar was assassinated he was about the same age as Robert E. Lee at Gettysburg. At Antietam, General McClellan was the same age as Napoleon at Austerlitz. Careers which, when we look back on them, seem to fill a long period of history, often fill only a few years.

Perhaps Americans are less conscious of this because of an historical accident in their own history. We all know that John Adams and Thomas Jefferson died on the fiftieth anniversary of the Declaration of Independence. We all know that Clay and Calhoun and Webster lived to be as old as General Eisenhower was when he left the White House. We all know that Martin Van Buren was the first President of the United States not born a British subject.

Because of this, many Americans, including many Americans in high office and many great political preachers, seem to me rather like Rip van Winkle. They come out of a long slumber and adjust rather slowly to the fact that King George has gone and has been replaced by George Washington. They notice the change on the inn sign, but are reluctant to notice more than that.

What follows from this perhaps platitudinous discourse and the fact 'crabbèd age and youth cannot live together'? What follows is extremely important. Habits of political judgement may long survive their utility. Generals are always reproached for planning to fight the last war; but Secretaries of State and Presidents can be reproached with fighting the last political war or living on the stock of knowledge and the stock of principles that served them well long before nearly half the voters of today were born.

I would not argue that all things must be made new. I would not argue that it is impossible to discern the permanent interests of the United States. I believe, for instance, that it is a permanent interest of the United States to prevent the establishment in either of the Americas of a great hostile military power. In that sense, the Monroe Doctrine is as valid today as when it was enunciated, with the important addition that now the United States can enforce the Monroe Doctrine more successfully than it could have done when President Monroe and Secretary Adams declared it to an uncandid and shocked world. But it may be a mistake to regard a Communist Cuba, still more a Communist Guiana or even a Communist Dominican Republic as a menace to the peace and good order of the Americas. The Latin American powers who refuse to rally with sufficient enthusiasm to North American clarion calls to action, even to negative political economic action, may not be hostile to the United States. They may simply think the United States is showing too much fright at shadows.

Many diplomatic historians have pointed out errors made by great powers in continuing to fear once dangerous rivals who had ceased to be rivals. For example, the Protectorate of Oliver Cromwell feared Spain, but not France. For a great part of her reign, the statesmen of Queen Victoria feared France and not Germany. It may be that the United States should give up fearing Russia, or even give up fearing Communism, and consider its relations with China as calling for the utmost vigilance and the least possible sentimentality, but not for panic and not for the application of a rigid and unalterable doctrine.

It may well be that in the next generation whatever happens in China will be the most important event in human history for many hundreds of years. If a modern, technological, unified Chinese state is created and is durable, it may be that the United States and Russia will be driven together; that doctrinal differences will seem as trivial in a few years' time as Christian doctrines seemed to Francis I of France when he allied himself with the Sultan against the Holy Roman Empire. And one is tempted if one is asked (and I have been asked) to talk to State Department officials, to give the advice that Talleyrand gave to young French diplomats, '*Surtout, pas trop de zèle*', or, in modern American, 'Above all, keep your cool.'

For reasons I have given earlier, this unideological, unemotional, selfish—if you like, unethical—attitude to foreign policy comes hard to the Americans. As I have already suggested, it comes hard for two reasons. The United States has been able to afford, first of all to have no foreign policy at all, and then to have a foreign policy which could be highly ideological, ethical, worthy of world admiration—at any rate as seen by Americans. It was not only, as the proverb puts it, 'God looks after drunks, children, and the United States'. The United States, less than most countries, needs the help of God in whom it professes its trust. This makes Americans, seen from the outside, seem brash and dogmatic, and leads many people to think that they are victims of their own moral rhetoric. But this abandonment of the evangelistic approach to world affairs —I am using evangelistic in no specific Christian sense— comes hardest to those who have lived through and been affected by two great crusades, the American rôle in the First and Second World Wars. It is true that Roosevelt determinedly played down the excessively moralistic, the excessively sermonizing tone in which Woodrow Wilson conducted American foreign policy. (It is a matter of debate among historians whether Wilson did not also pursue the natural interests of the United States in saving the Atlantic from German domination as well as the democratic system which Germany was alleged to threaten; but this is an historical question of no great relevance here.)

But long before the United States was thrust into the war by the folly of Japan, and then of Germany and Italy, the American people had ceased to be neutral in thought, and their government had ceased to be neutral in fact. Seen from the outside, Pearl Harbor got Roosevelt 'off the hook'. But the belief that it brought the United States in, only somewhat sooner than the nature of things would have done, does not minimize the importance of the speed with which the United States *was* brought into the war. It *may* have brought about the fall of the Axis. American intervention a year later might have been too late. *But* in a negative way, the Second World War was, for the American people, a crusade as much as the First. Hitler, after all, was much more obviously a real monster, someone issued from Hell, than the foolish, hysterical, but not basically wicked Kaiser ever was. Hitler's Reich was what Gladstone said of the kingdom of Naples, 'the negation of God erected into a system of government'. The destruction of Hitlerism, if only a negative achievement, was yet an achievement which had a high moral value and which was in fact a necessity for any improvement in the political morality of the whole world.

Imperial Japan was obviously a danger to the peace and well-being of Asia, and I think there is no doubt that for a great many of the American people, the war against Japan which had inflicted on the United States the greatest humiliation in its history, Pearl Harbor, was emotionally more satisfying than the war against Germany. But if crusades are ever justified, and if there is a black and white antithesis between states, the war against the Third Reich was a justifiable crusade and a legitimate moral judgement on the spirit of the Third Reich whose doctrines were as devilish as its practice.

But two crusades, each ending in military victory, each in a sense doing what they set out to do negatively, yet have left the American people disillusioned with crusades, or with crusades not carried to a totally successful conclusion, so that in the public mind of the United States today there is either a renewed disillusionment with the hopes which went, for example, to the foundation of the United States, or a possibly unconscious readiness to keep on crusading, a readiness that very few nations of the world today share, and which very few rulers of the world share except, possibly, the rulers of Communist China.

One illusion which lingers on in the American mind, or at any rate in the mind of some noisy Americans and, more quietly, in the mind of some elderly Americans, is that the Bolshevik Revolution either did not take place or is a transitory as well as an evil phenomenon. It is as well to remember that two years from now, that revolution will be fifty years old. The same space of time will have passed from the storming of the Winter Palace in Petrograd as passed between the Declaration of Independence and the deaths of John Adams and Thomas Jefferson. Even the most rabid hater of the revolutionary republic across the Atlantic did not, in 1826, expect to see it collapse and be replaced by a loyal British colony or even a set of loyal British colonies. Many people in Europe anticipated, many people in Europe hoped, many people in Europe feared that the Union would break up. Many Americans shared the fear, if few shared the hope. And the United States was to undergo a trial seldom equalled in history, so that the fears were not totally unjustified although the hopes proved to be justified. In the same way, one must accept the fact that whatever happens in Russia (we ignore for the moment the pedantry of calling that great state the Union of Soviet Socialist Republics), the Bolshevik Revolution has happened. 'The Revolution has happened' is what Napoleon used to say to people who tried to evade the consequences of the overthrow of the French monarchy—he was sometimes a Jacobin in spirit as he had been a Jacobin in fact; but even when he was by marriage a kinsman of the last King of France, he never had any illusions about the greatness of the event which had dethroned and executed his wife's uncle and had made it possible for him to mount the vacant throne.

In the same way, Americans, indeed all observers, of the modern world must repeatedly say to themselves, if they have any romantic waverings in their mind, 'The Bolshevik Revolution has happened'. It has endured for fifty years. It is convenient in face of some naïve comments of left-wing propaganda to point out that the triumph of the Bolsheviks was not anticipated, that but for the First World War and, possibly, but for the pathological incompetence of the last Czar, some other adjustment, some other profound change in the seized-up imperial machine would have occurred, but that power would not have passed to a group of internal and external conspirators whose leader V. I. Lenin, in exile, despaired of seeing his cause triumph in his own lifetime just before it did.[1]

[1] There is a story whose authenticity is perhaps questionable that the Bolshevik leaders in Petrograd were overwhelmed with joy when

These essays in hypothetical history can be justified since they save us from the servility of believing that what has happened is the only possible thing that could have happened. In that sense, they are sometimes useful guides to action as well as prophylactics against the credulous acceptance of what has happened. There are and always will be men, some of them very intelligent, who will accept as the wave of the future what is in fact a wave which will soon recede. There are others who, in fact, identify a wave of the future correctly, but are not very good guides to what the future is to be. But when all these intellectual precautions are taken, we must come back, as Napoleon came back again and again, to the fact that the Bolshevik Revolution has happened and that the history of the world will never be the same again. This will probably be accepted by most Americans under the age of fifty, even if a good many Americans under fifty deplore it as the most disastrous event in human history since the Fall, indeed regard it as the *real* Fall. But this intellectual assent does not colour the mind adequately to prevent certain illusions having a disastrous influence. It is not enough to accept the fact that the Bolshevik Revolution happened. We must accept the fact that for many millions of people fifty years ago, and much more recently, the Russian Revolution in general, the Communist Revolution in particular, was what the Fall of the Bastille was for Charles James Fox:

> How much the greatest event it is that ever happened in the world! And how much the best!

Even today, there are many pilgrims who go to Moscow as devout Muslims went and still go to Mecca. The Red Star

they realized that their experimental revolution had lasted a day longer than the Paris Commune of 1871. This story, if true, suggests that Lenin, even formally in power in the Smolny, did not see himself as the predestined ruler of Russia, as the chosen instrument of the Dialectic.

over the Kremlin, the tomb of Lenin: these are symbols of achievement and symbols of hope. Even the empty grave of Stalin does not destroy their faith.

To repeat myself, the Russian Revolution was the culmination of a century of hopes and a century of hates. The history of the Western world for many millions of people had been a series of defeats: the defeat of the Revolution of 1848; of the Paris Commune of 1871; of a series of great and bloody strikes in the United States; of what they thought the judicial murder of the Haymarket anarchists in Chicago; a history in Russia of pogroms, revolts and an abortive triumph in 1905. Now, in one of the greatest states in the world, 'la lutte finale'—the final struggle sung in the great revolutionary anthem, the 'Internationale'—had begun, and begun with victory. Not God, but the ineluctable movement of history had 'put down the mighty from their seats and exalted them of low degree'. It had 'filled the hungry with good things, and the rich had sent empty away'. Even the fact that the hungry had not been filled with good things did not totally offset the fact that the rich *had* been sent empty away.

The generations of hostility to bourgeois society, the dislike that many millions felt for the triumphs of Western capitalist society celebrated in prose and verse, if not in poetry, by so many popular authors in Britain and in America, had prepared a world audience for the news of the 'ten days that shook the world', as John Reed put it.

No doubt for most of Western Europe and for most of North America, even including Mexico in North America, these hopeful illusions are over. No doubt capitalist society has shown fresh resources and has in fact done a good deal towards feeding the hungry if very little about sending the rich empty away. But for most of the world the desire not to be hungry as so many generations have been or, if hunger must remain, to make sure it is shared by everyone—'a joy in widest commonalty spread', as the once revolutionary poet Wordsworth put it—remains. That this passion to end physical hunger or, if not, to make sure that, if the meek do not inherit the earth, no one else will, makes a great deal of our automatic reactions to the overwhelming majority of the world foolish and dangerous. We may not think any longer, as did Dickens's Mrs. Jellyby, of 'educating the natives of Borrioboola-Gha, on the left bank of the Niger', but a great deal of American propaganda, a great deal of American puzzlement at the failure of the propaganda, arises from the survival of the idea that there is a market for Mrs. Jellyby's Christianity and for the political ethics of George Horace Lorimer's *Letters of a Self-made Merchant to his Son*, to recall a now-forgotten Philadelphian author who was treated as seriously in his lifetime as Benjamin Franklin had been in his.

For this reason, the Communists can draw on a great deal of resentment, a great deal of hatred, a great deal of admiration and, especially where they are not at hand, a great deal of love. They can also draw on a genuine passion for 'the general welfare' among many of the best and most promising young men and women as well, of course, as on the naïve hatred and ambition of some of the worst.

Just as it would be absurd to condemn many of the Abolitionists by pointing out how their zeal was exploited by some highly unethical characters like Senator Simon Cameron; just as it would be inadequate to point out that John Brown was a visible paranoiac and thus explain the spirit behind the writing and singing of either 'John Brown's Body' or the 'Battle Hymn of the Republic'; so it is absurd to ignore the genuine faith, hope, if not charity, behind the singing of the 'Internationale' and behind the liberating forces of the hammer-and-sickle as seen by spokesmen for the vast, depressed masses of the world. It is too easy and too dangerous to point out that these hopes are often illusory and that the last state of the poor will be worse than the first. For one thing, this is not always true. There is no reason to believe, for instance, that the inhabitants of what used to be called Russian Central Asia are worse off than the subjects of the Shah. But above all we must remember that our power of empathy with the vast masses of Asia and Africa, to whom Communism can make an appeal, if often a dishonest appeal, and our ability to win men of goodwill even if of naïve political judgement, are very limited. We ought to repeat to ourselves, 'No hungry generations tread *us* down.'[1]

If it is difficult to ask men and women who can remember the world of the First World War and even the world just before the Second World War, to accept the fact that a great revolutionary situation has been stabilized with the survival of the Soviet Union, it is far harder to get most people of any age in the West to accept the fact that a great, inexorable revolution is going on nearly all over the world. In a way, the fall of the Czardom was a model revolution in the old European and American tradition. The Czar was *the* tyrant by definition. Did he not call himself 'the Autocrat'? Ever since the French Revolution, the Czardom had been seen blocking the way to the liberation of Europe. Despite occasional fleeting moments of popularity, such as the friendly relations established between the Union and the Czardom during the American Civil War, the Russian Empire was the embodiment of political evil, or at any rate of political backwardness. The oppression of Poland by the Russians, and the oppression of Ireland by the English, were standard examples of imperialist tyranny used by radicals all over Europe and all over North America. (Even the most zealous Irishman would,

[1] Whether a person, like myself, of Irish origin can do this is a matter for historians to debate. For the Irish seem to fall into two classes: the descendants of dethroned kings or the descendants of victims of the famine; but both these beliefs are often legends, and that has nothing to do with their political effect!

if pressed, have admitted there were slight superiorities on the side of the English tyrant over the Russian one!) Russian military power had been used to crush the freedom of Hungary in 1849. (Few foresaw that Russian military power would be used over a hundred years later for exactly the same ends: the destruction of political freedom in Hungary.)

At a time when anti-Semitism was thought to be a sign of backward and barbarous countries, it was the Russian empire that was the great stronghold of anti-Semitism. It legislated against the Jews as such; it tolerated and, indeed, fostered, outbursts of anti-Semitic violence which acquired the generic name of pogroms.[1]

Nationalist minorities, of whom the Poles were only the most numerous, conspired more or less openly against Russian imperial rule. The semi-independent Grand Duchy of Finland was under constant Russian pressure directed to diminish its guaranteed liberties. The repeated assassinations of great Russian officials—Grand Dukes and Governors-General—were received with applause by many people in Europe and America, and with a tolerant understanding by most of the rest. The victory of Japan over Russia (so full of consequences for the West) was regarded as the victory of a progressive and increasingly respectable state over a backward and possibly regressive state. The faint hopes put in the liberalism of Czar Alexander II, the Liberator of the Serfs, had been crushed under his son and grandson, Alexander III and Nicholas II. The picture of Russian rule accepted by most of what was then thought of as the civilized world was painted by enemies, exiles—by people like Prince Kropotkin, the

[1] I can remember being in a watchmaker's shop in Glasgow during the First War, and the customers discussing the cause of the war. A Jewish immigrant said, 'I always remember that Germany is a constitutional and law-abiding state, and Russia is not'. Millions of his kinsfolk were to learn that he was in error!

great anarchist philosopher, in the brilliant and embittered novel of Joseph Conrad, *Under Western Eyes*. This anti-Russian theme can be found even among the cases of Sherlock Holmes! The failure of the Revolution of 1905 was regretted by most people in the West, and when the Duma was dissolved by the Czar, the new British Prime Minister, Sir Henry Campbell-Bannerman, at a great international assembly in London gave the toast, 'La Douma est morte; vive la Douma'. Even that flibbertigibbet William II of Germany, devoted as he professed to be to his first cousin Nicholas II, was quite capable of trying to exploit in his trivial way Polish dislike of Russian rule. So that psychologically speaking the West was well prepared for *a* Russian revolution, and the fact that the Russian revolution which triumphed was not a liberal revolution was ignored or concealed by many zealous and by many sentimental liberals for whom the overthrow of the Czardom had been a dream and a promise for over a century.[1]

It was natural that the millions of Jews of fairly recent or immediate Russian origin should not be critical of any movement that brought down the Czardom. German rule in the Russian territories occupied by the Germans in the First World War had been an improvement on Russian rule, although it was a short-lived occupation. The fall of the Czardom made possible the creation not only of a liberated Poland, but of a liberated Esthonia, Latvia and Lithuania. After a bloody civil war, it secured the complete independence of Finland. So it was quite natural that the truth, the increasingly depressing truth, about Stalin's Russia should have been concealed or evaded, especially in wartime when Stalin was an extremely valuable if

[1] The well-known Philadelphia soap manufacturer, Mr. Joseph Fels, had innocently lent money to Lenin whom he regarded as one of the numerous liberal leaders he had a duty to subsidize, and when Lenin eventually took over Russia, Mr. Fels, in all simplicity, asked for his money back. Lenin sent it back.

dangerous ally. These illusions are nearly all dead. Whatever the Soviet Union is today, it is not automatically a star of hope for Left-wing movements in Europe or in America. Indeed, the most hopeful view of the Soviet Union is that it is ceasing to be revolutionary and is settling down more as an inferior copy of the United States than as the model of the future that Lincoln Steffens thought it was.

But when we turn to the rest of the world and to a revolutionary situation that shows no signs of settling down, it is far harder for the West, especially for the Americans, to adjust to the changes. To repeat, it is possible that, but for the Second World War, the political and economic and social evolution of Russia, Asia and Latin America would have been much slower. It might also have been much happier. But the Second World War brought down the great European empires of Asia—the British, French and Dutch. It was soon to do the same for the British, French and Belgian empires in Africa. It was soon to threaten the leadership of the United States in the Americas. Even if there had been no ideological campaign against the West, the mere multiplication on a great scale of the shock given to white superiority by the defeat of Russia in 1905 would have created a revolutionary situation and a revolutionary problem.[1]

But of course there was an ideological element in the new revolutionary situation. In Asia and Africa, it was no longer a matter of blind revolt, an equivalent of the peasant revolts of medieval Europe and indeed of Russia down to quite modern times. The new revolutionary movements in Asia and Africa differed as much from the futile attempts to

[1] I myself showed no foresight on this question, for in a book I wrote during the Second War, *The English People*, I greatly underestimated the degree to which the declining imperial structures in Asia were being shaken into ruins, and I ignored the process in Africa almost entirely.

resist white supremacy of the nineteenth century as the Russian Revolution of 1917 differed from the various attempts to bring to power in Russia the *real* Czar instead of the usurper deemed to be on the throne, or to liberate the Czar from the wicked counsellors who came between him and his peoples. If the Manchu dynasty was visibly exhausting its 'mandate of heaven', it was not a question of waiting for a new dynasty (how hopeless an enterprise was the attempt in 1916 of Yüan Shih-k'ai to set himself up as the new Son of Heaven!). Ideas were loose all over Asia and all over Africa. And, these ideas were not the simple, safe, and Western ideas of American or European liberalism.

It was not only a matter, or perhaps mainly a matter, of the active intervention of the new Soviet government in the internal politics of China, not a matter of deals with the rising young general Chiang Kai-shek. It was not a matter in India of being merely slightly more uncompromising in opposition to British rule. The idea that society could be reconstructed from top to bottom, the idea that this had been done in Russia and with great success, materially and psychologically, was not in itself an absurd idea, and certainly was a great spur to action.

It is not surprising, indeed, that 'Communism', however vaguely this term may be interpreted, spread all over Asia and Africa. It is more surprising that it did not spread faster and did not strike deeper roots. The Western observer, inclined to be superior and censorious (this is especially true, I fear, of the American Western observer), has to tell himself again and again that nothing was more natural and in many ways more admirable than the turning towards the rising sun of Communism of so many of the most admirable young men and young women in China, Japan, India—all over the under-privileged world. Faced with the situation in Shanghai; faced with the sight of the Calcutta slums; faced with the taking over of the Japanese government by militarists whose answer to extremely real economic and social problems was literally and inevitably dangerous, it is no wonder that Communism recruited men and women in many nations.

It is a hard saying, but it has to be said. In these countries, Communism in its Russian or, most recently, its Chinese form has had a power of attraction both of some of the best elements among the young and of the most formidable elements among the young, that has been constantly underestimated, especially in the United States. There was, and indeed there is, nothing unnatural in warm-hearted if not necessarily clear-headed young men and young women in Brazil, Japan, India, Iran, seeing in Communism the only force that can break 'the cake of custom', the only force that can pull backward societies, suffering visibly from immense and centuries-old evils, into the modern world where a new way of life is possible.

It is therefore foolish of official Americans or unofficial Americans, politicians, professors or journalists, to assess the weight, the effectiveness and the efficacy of the various leaders establishing their rule in Asia, Africa and Latin America by their degree of fidelity to the United States or to 'the American way of life', or to Christianity or, indeed, to theism. These potential leaders or these actual leaders must be assessed in terms of their own countries' needs and their own countries' illusions. These leaders cannot be simply conjured out of the earth by the most massive doses of military or straight economic aid. If these sick societies are to remain in the eyes of the most energetic inhabitants of the countries sick, possibly incurable except by violent and dangerous operations, this is a political condition which must be assessed calmly with as little moralistic emotion as is humanly possible.

This is not to say that human emotion has no place. The human emotion of charity has a great place. The human emotion of promoting the vast world interests of the

United States has and should have a great place. What those basic interests are at any given moment will be a matter of debate. Not even the most faithful allies of the United States will always see eye to eye with what the current American assumption of American interests is; nor in every instance can it be guaranteed that American and British or French or German interests *are* identical.

Something of the patience that Woodrow Wilson showed in the face of the disorder, violence, crime of the Mexican revolution is called for today. Who can doubt that he was right in not pinning all his hopes on armed American intervention? Who can doubt that a merely military victory may be sterile and may not last much longer than victory normally does? Who can doubt that it will be difficult to keep up the crusading atmosphere of the Cold War into the next generation, although there is every reason to believe that the problems which were summed up under the title 'the Cold War' will remain, will be equally serious even if we cannot foresee the exact character or the range of solutions open to the United States or to the West in general?

There are a few things which can with some confidence be predicted. The first is that all detailed predictions will certainly be, in detail, wrong. History has its record of very successful general predictions. Burke foresaw that the French Revolution would end in the rule of a soldier dictator. But he could not have foreseen—who could?—that the dictator would be such a prodigy of history as Napoleon Bonaparte. It would probably have been safe to bet both on the concentration of power in one man under Communist rule in Russia and to suggest that the heir of Lenin would again be one man and not a committee. (It can be debated whether Stalin was a legitimate heir of Lenin or not; I think he was.) But the organization of the Communist Party and the needs of the Communist dictatorship would almost certainly have produced someone fulfilling the main office of Stalin, although it is reasonable to hope in a less barbarously and extravagantly murderous way.

The record of political prophecy in this century has not been good. Too many hopes have been raised only to be deceived. So that the conviction that we do not know in detail even the immediate future and that we should be very rash to plan as if we did, is a sceptical truth worth emphasizing. Perhaps things *should* be different. But I have some prejudice against this style of argument and this style of rhetoric. We should remember the wise counsel of Bishop Butler: 'Things and actions are what they are, and the consequences of them will be what they will be: why then should we desire to be deceived?' Such an attitude does not come naturally to the American mind or live comfortably in the American mind, but that is the way the world wags all the same. We should remember that the power of organized prediction is no better on the other side of the hill than on ours. Errors of judgement made by Stalin are quite as startling as any made by any Western statesman or politician. 'The great leap forward' was not a very visible success in China, and we must remember that the very survival of a régime in itself is proof of only one kind of success—survival, not of the success of the programme produced by the political survivors. Chairman Mao is an old man, and it may be that the China which he has transformed more than any ruler in Chinese history since legendary times will not prove satisfactory to his successors and perhaps is already proving to some degree unsatisfactory to him.

The very success of American policy in fostering the economic recovery of Europe shows the dangers of prophesying, for a great many people who were not in the least pro-Communist greatly doubted the possibility of salvaging Europe after the last war.[1]

[1] Since I have several times commented on my lack of prophetic power, I *may* say that I never shared this pessimistic belief about European recovery even in the dark days of 1945–8.

Then we must be prepared to allow not only for unpleasant technical developments, but for unforeseen results of technical and political developments. For change, even successful change, forces other changes or creates new problems. I can remember the comments made by a Dutch efficiency expert before the last war on the difficulties of reorganizing French business. The trouble was, he said, that the French were too clever, and that a year after the business had been reorganized according to his plan, everybody in the French firm, from the head of it down to the office boy, had suggested and acted on improvements, all of which *were* improvements but nevertheless wrecked the plan. Perhaps Walter Bagehot was right, and one of the reasons for the comparative political sense of the English is their stupidity!

Then, Americans and all the West must remember that there is a great danger of a great part of the world not slowly following in their footsteps, but going backwards. Modern 'advanced' political and technological society is a very fragile structure, even in the countries where it has natural foundations. The immunity to which we have long been accustomed in the West to such great catastrophes as universal famine, plague, devastating earthquakes (the last is a purely geological virtue) is not so far shared by the greater part of the human race. It is brutal, but not necessarily foolish, to regret, in the face of the population explosion, the success of science in getting down the infantile death rate in India and Latin America. Faced by such a challenge, we should do everything (that includes providing the means of the control of conceptions, familiarly called birth control) to reduce the pressures of the population explosion. Even so great a gain as the saving of the lives of many millions of babies has a very high economic and political price.

We do not know how soon, or even if it will be in this century, that the political stability of what we call freedom can be established in Africa or in a great part of Latin America. We cannot guarantee that fragile political structures like the present governmental system in Iran or in the Arab states will survive for even a decade, and the rôle of official fomenters of revolution like the Chinese Communists may not matter one way or the other. On the other hand, it is too easy and too complacent, too much a sign of the white man's sense of superiority, to assume that adequate solutions which are not ours may not be found for political and economic and social problems of Asia and Africa. There may be some meaning of material value in the concept of *Négritude*. It may be that Islam will prove an effective religious framework for necessary revolutionary changes in the Arab world. It may be that in the race between salvation and catastrophe, the heirs of Nehru may win. It is right and desirable to be hopeful as long as we remember that there is a race, and that it is, in the American sense of the term, a horse race.

We can be quite sure that a great many of the problems and a great many of the traditional feuds and historical memories all over the world will change their character in the next two or three decades. The world of 2000 will be very different from the world of 1965, and it may well be very much better, but there is no guarantee that this will be so. Europe has twice in this century shown all the follies very advanced societies are capable of, and these, it must be remembered, were political follies. There is some reason to be afraid that the new 'nations' coming to birth, sometimes only after painful Caesarean operations, may imitate the violence of Europe more successfully than its few examples of wisdom. I have no doubt that the main obstacle to the conquest of the under-privileged regions of the world is, in fact, nationalism in some form or other. The Chinese and the Russians cannot help behaving as the Western whites have behaved for so long, with a humiliating attitude of being teachers. They cannot help behaving, as Chesterton described Matthew Arnold as behaving, with the tired patience of a teacher in an idiot school. But the world is not in fact an idiot school. Even the most backward parts of it—backward in the technological sense—are not populated by idiots, but by human beings who have all the possibilities of our progress before them although many things, including their own past history, may prevent the full attainment of that promise.

Every day and in every way the world gets, not better and better, but more and more complicated or, if you like, curiouser and curiouser. There is no divinely ordained caucus race in which every competitor gets a prize. But the prizes open to the whole world are, in terms of material well-being, unprecedented in human experience. The underprivileged peoples or, if you like, the technologically backward peoples may suffer a double disappointment: the almost certain disappointment that they will not overtake the technologically advanced peoples in the next generation, and they may also suffer the more poignant disappointment of finding their material condition not better, but in many ways worse, not only through the population explosion, but by the decline of their economic bargaining position in the world. They may even suffer another form of backwardness, of losing their faith in their old institutions and traditions without acquiring any very deep faith in the new institutions which various leading nations—the United States, the Soviet Union, China—try to sell them.

But it would be against my belief, as well as against my hopes, to end on a note of mere pessimism. I *do* want to end on a note of warning. The West can never face the rest of the world in its old spirit of confident superiority. For us, it will never be 'bright confident morning' again. But our power of promoting our own and the world's general welfare has, on a material level, never before been so great. Yet material power and even technical knowledge are not all that is needed. James Conant, a very distinguished scientist and former President of Harvard (he has held many other lesser offices), was wise in saying that what the United States needs is not more brilliant scientists, but more statemen of the calibre of men like James Madison. The rest of the 'advanced' world is in the same situation. Moscow and Peking need wisdom quite as much as does London or Paris or Washington. The state which has the greatest power, the greatest wealth and, on the whole, the greatest fund of goodwill on which to draw is the United States. But its power of doing good is limited by certain psychological barriers and certain historical illusions. If I were asked to give advice to any American statesman or, indeed, to the whole American people, I should be inclined to take my text from *Don Quixote* and say with the priest, 'Patience, and shuffle the cards'. The American cards are numerous and excellent; it is the patience that has been and is too often lacking. Many of the problems with us today will be with our children and our grandchildren. There are no political 'Rock Candy Mountains'. The Declaration of Independence and the Constitution are aimed at the future, at a state of perfection not to be reached at once or, indeed, perhaps ever in human history. And this means that the American stock of preserved ideas must be continually examined and a good deal of the contents continuously discarded. This weighs no more heavily on the Americans than on the British, the French, the Germans, the Russians. But it weighs no less heavily. And it is perhaps the most difficult and necessary burden for the American man and woman to accept. We must all accept the truth of the impossibility of escaping from our historical destiny into either daydreams or a passionate, outrageous break with reality.

'Tis true there's better booze than brine,
But he that drowns must drink it,
And oh my lass, the news is news
That men have heard before.

We need, all of the West needs, some of this Spartan acceptance of the inevitable tragedy of most of human existence.